Donated To

Johnson Library

By

Mrs. Gail Howell

Investigating Science in the Swimming Pool and Ocean

Investigating Science in the Swimming Pool and Ocean

by *Norman D. Anderson*

illustrated by Steve Daniels

MCGRAW-HILL BOOK COMPANY

New York St. Louis San Francisco Auckland Bogotá
Düsseldorf Johannesburg London Madrid Mexico Montreal
New Delhi Panama Paris São Paulo Singapore
Sydney Tokyo Toronto

Library of Congress Cataloging in Publication Data

Anderson, Norman D.
  Investigating science in the swimming pool and ocean.

  SUMMARY: Instructions for experiments with water investigating
such questions as why some objects float, how can water depth be
measured, and other related topics.
  1. Science—Juvenile literature. 2. Water—
Juvenile literature. [1. Water—Experiments.
2. Science—Experiments. 3. Experiments]
I. Daniels, Steve. II. Title.
Q163.A55   530'.028   77-27241
ISBN 0-07-001634-8

Contents

Acknowledgments

THE IDEA for this book came from watching one of my children playing in a swimming pool. And once I decided to write the book, the family came up with all kinds of great ideas. For this and their help in trying out experiments, I am deeply grateful.

Thanks also go to the many students at North Carolina State University who suggested investigations. And a special thank you to Judy Spitsbergen and Joanne Powell of the Mariners Museum in Beaufort, North Carolina for their ideas and suggestions.

9

Introduction

A GROUP of teenagers stands near the diving boards talking about an upcoming swimming meet. Several people are swimming laps in the part of the pool marked off in lanes. At the shallow end of the pool several young people are in the middle of a water fight.

Two of the young people, however, are not interested in getting drenched in the big battle. Instead, they are more interested in playing with a large plastic ball. First one and then the other holds the ball underwater and then releases it. The ball rises rapidly to the surface and shoots into the air! The idea of the game is to see who can make the ball go the highest.

It was while I watched a group of young people at a swimming pool that the idea of this book was born. The game with the ball involves a great deal of science. What makes the ball float? Why was it necessary to push down on the ball to hold it under the water? What force pushes the ball into the air? Since one of the big ideas of science is prediction, suggest as many ways as you can to make a ball go higher.

In looking around the swimming pool, it is easy to see many other principles of science in action. A boy stands on an air mattress. When he jumps forward into the water, the air mattress shoots backward. No doubt about it—Newton's Third Law of Motion works as well in the swimming pool as in the science laboratory.

At the far end of the pool, two divers stand poised on twin diving boards. The boy on the left board surely weighs half again as much as the girl on the right. What happens when they both jump at the same instant? Will the heavier boy reach the water first?

Have you ever had an idea and then forgotten about it, only to have it occur to you again sometime later? So it was with the many examples of science that I observed in a swimming pool.

A few weeks later, while I was vacationing at the beach, more ideas came to mind. Swimming pools are not the only place to do investigations involving water. What makes a beach chair sink when a wave wets the sand on which it is placed? If you are standing in the surf, when do your feet sink most rapidly? When the wave is coming in or when the water is running back toward the ocean?

If you try floating on an air mattress when the surf is breaking, you are pounded by the crashing waves and often upset. However, if you paddle out beyond the breakers, the air mattress peacefully bobs up and down. What does this tell you about waves?

Everywhere there seemed to be examples of science involving water. And so the ideas for this book grew and grew.

All of the investigations described in this book can be carried out in or near the water. Some work best in clear water, like in a swimming pool, pond, or lake. Others require a larger body of water, such as a lake or an ocean, on which there are waves. A few can be done in a river. Those dealing with salt water and tides are best done at the seashore.

You don't have access to a swimming pool, pond, river, lake, or ocean? Or it is too cold outside to carry out experiments in the water? No problem: many of the investigations can be done in a bathtub or the kitchen sink. A few can even be performed in a body of water as small as a drinking glass.

Sometimes the directions suggest ways you can do the investigations using more than one approach. In other cases you may have to improvise in order to do the investigation inside your house. Improvising, of course, is half the fun of exploring science.

You won't need a lot of equipment to do these investigations. Much of it you already have or can borrow—things like beach balls, air mattresses, and plastic pails. You also can improvise when it comes to equipment. A large plastic milk container with part of the top cut off works fine as a pail. A large piece of Styrofoam makes almost as good a raft as does an air mattress.

The measurements given in this book are in inches, feet, ounces, pounds, quarts, gallons, etc. The reason these units are used is that most common household equipment you will be using is marked off in these units of measurement. In addition, the metric equivalents of most measurements have been included in parentheses. A list of commonly used metric units is included in the Appendix, along with directions for converting from one system of measurement to the other.

Care has been taken to make the directions as helpful as possible. But the directions for science investigations are like the recipes in a cookbook. Even though you follow the directions carefully, your results may not be exactly what you expected. If this happens, don't let it discourage you. Neither a science investigation nor the recipe for a chocolate cake may turn out right the first time. Repeat the investigation if you are not satisfied with your results. And try to figure out what may be going wrong. The "thinking" part of an investigation is one of the most important parts of science.

Most of the investigations in this book in some way involve water. Therefore all the usual *safety precautions* taken when working or playing around water should be observed. For example, you should always practice the "buddy system." This means not going in or near the water by yourself. You should always be with a "buddy," and preferably someone who is a good swimmer.

Don't take chances. Wear a life preserver when you work from a boat or are near deep water.

If you do your investigations in a swimming pool, it first will be necessary to get permission from the owner, the manager, or one of the lifeguards. They will insist that you use only plastic or wooden equipment—no glass! Glass containers are dangerous because they may break and cause injuries.

Are you ready to get started? If so, put on your swimming suit. You will have to get into the water to do many of the investigations described in the next section.

Swimming Pool Physics

PHYSICS IS THE BRANCH of science that deals with matter and energy. This includes how and why things move, why some things float, and what causes pressure. The many kinds of energy studied in physics include sound, light, and heat. Some of these energy forms are best studied using water.

Let's start with the problem of a beach ball. What makes it fly into the air when it is held underwater and released? To answer this question, we must first answer another question. Why does the ball float?

WHY DO SOME OBJECTS FLOAT?

When you place a beach ball or basketball in water, it floats. However, if you observe carefully, you will notice it doesn't float on top of the water. Instead, it sinks partway into the water. The ball displaces, or pushes out of the way, some water. Figure 1 shows the approximate amount of water displaced by a basketball.

The displacement of water by a floating object can be easily observed in a drinking glass. Fill the glass about half full with water. Mark the level of the water on the side of the glass. Now add an ice cube. The

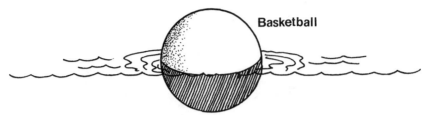

Figure 1. The shaded area represents the amount of water displaced by the floating basketball.

level of the water in the glass rises because the floating ice cube displaces some of the water.

Need another example of displacement? The next time you take a bath, notice what happens when you lower yourself into the tub of water. How does the level of the water change?

Explaining why an object floats is related to how much water it displaces. This idea can be easily investigated using simple equipment. Let's use a paper milk carton, a paper cup, a scale, a small ball that floats, and some water.

The first step is to weigh the ball. A food scale or postage scale will work fine. Write down the weight on a piece of paper. Keeping good records is always an important part of doing investigations in science.

Next, cut the top of the milk carton off. Now cut a slot on either side of one corner of the carton. Bend the corner down to form a spout, as shown in Figure 2.

Fill the carton with water so the level is even with the spout. Weigh the paper cup and then place it under the spout. Next, slowly lower the ball into the carton.

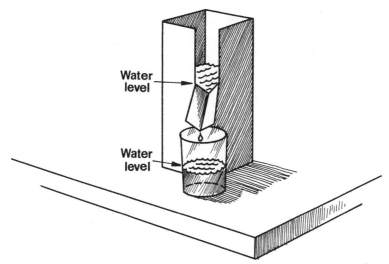

Figure 2. *This device used to study floating objects can be made from a milk carton.*

The water displaced by the ball will flow down the spout and into the cup.

Now weigh the cup again. Subtract the weight of the empty cup from the weight of the cup of water. This tells you the weight of the water displaced by the ball. Do you see why?

Compare the weight of the ball with the weight of the water displaced by the ball. Although they may not be exactly equal, they should be about the same. This gives us a clue to why something floats. *An object floats when it displaces an amount of water equal to its weight.*

This explanation of floating applies to all floating objects—beach balls, people, and even supertankers.

If a beach ball weighs a pound (0.45 kilograms), it displaces a pound of water when it floats. If you weigh 120 pounds (54 kilograms), you displace 120 pounds of water when you float. A supertanker is described as having a displacement of several hundred thousand tons because this is about as much water as it displaces.

TIME OUT TO IMPROVISE

Stop! You say you don't have a scale to weigh the water? Remember what we said earlier about the fun of improvising? In this case, we can use the science of a playground seesaw to solve our problem. If two people of equal weight each sit equal distances from the center, the seesaw balances.

Figure 3 shows how to use this idea to weigh the water. Balance a ruler or a small wooden board on a pencil or other round object. Next place the ball inside a cup on one side. On the other side place a similar cup

Figure 3. A simple method of finding out if the ball and water weigh the same amount.

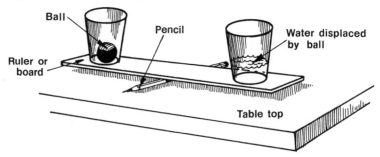

containing the water that was displaced by the floating ball.

Do you see why a cup is placed on each side of our tabletop seesaw? The one on the right, of course, is there to hold the water. But why one on the left? True, it does keep the ball from rolling off. However, there is another reason. The weight of the cup on the left balances the weight of the cup on the right. Thus, we can forget about the weight of the cups. If the cup holding the ball is the same distance from the center of the seesaw as the cup holding the water, we know the ball and water are the same weight. Can you figure out which is heavier if the two cups are not the same distance from the center?

Another method of weighing things is described on page 23.

Now let's get back to the problem we started out to solve—the mystery of the flying beach ball!

WHY DOES THE BEACH BALL FLY INTO THE AIR?

As we have seen, a beach ball floats in water only partly submerged. Try pushing down on a beach ball so it is completely submerged. It takes a force to hold the ball underwater. Let go of the ball and it flies into the air.

Scientists use the term *buoyancy* to explain floating and what happens when the ball is pushed under the water. Buoyancy is the upward force produced by the ball displacing the water. There also is a downward force on the ball. This is the ball's weight, which is the result of gravity pulling on the ball. When an object floats, the upward force of buoyancy is equal to the downward force on the object. When two forces are equal but in opposite directions, they cancel each other out. This is like a tug-of-war when each team is pulling an equal amount.

When the ball is pushed under the water, the upward force of buoyancy is greatly increased. This is because more water is displaced. The downward force of gravity on the ball, however, remains the same. Now what happens when one of the opposing forces is much greater than the other? What happens, of course, is the same thing that happens when one team in tug-of-war pulls with a greater force than the other team. In the case of the ball, it moves upward because the upward force of buoyancy is greater than the downward force of gravity.

HOW CAN YOU MAKE THE BALL GO EVEN HIGHER?

First try releasing the ball when you have pushed it down so it is only about half submerged. Next, compare how high it goes with the results you get when the ball is completely submerged and released. The greater the force of buoyancy on the ball, the higher it should go. Thus the completely submerged ball goes higher than the one only partly submerged.

Suppose a friend challenges you to a contest to see who can make a ball go higher. The rules you agree on state that you both have to use balls of the same size. What can you do to make the ball go higher and win the contest?

What do you predict would happen if one ball weighed more than the other one—for example, if one was a ball weighing a bit more than a pound, and the other was the same size, but made of plastic and weighing quite a bit less than a pound? Both balls displace the same amount of water when completely submerged. Thus they both have the same force of buoyancy pushing upward. However, the downward force of gravity is less for the plastic ball than for the heavier ball.

With most ideas in science, the best way to really understand something is by trying it. Try different kinds of balls or other objects. Do spherical objects like balls go higher than other shapes such as long sticks? If you can't try this in a swimming pool, lake, or the ocean, perhaps you can do your experiments in a bathtub or large sink.

We can use what we have learned about floating objects as a springboard to dozens of other investigations. As you read about the ones described in the rest of this chapter, see how many questions you can come up with yourself.

WHAT HAPPENS TO OBJECTS THAT DON'T FLOAT WHEN PLACED IN WATER?

One kind of cement block weighs about 30 pounds (13.5 kilograms). Would it be easier to lift one of these blocks on dry land or when it is in the water?

The next time you go swimming, try lifting some of your friends. First try it before they get into the water. Then try lifting them when they are partly submerged in the water. Then try it when they are completely submerged.

Even though an object may not float, something happens to how much it seems to weigh when it is placed in water. For example, a cement block seems to weigh less in water; this is so because the block displaces some water. You can investigate the amount of this weight loss by weighing some submerged objects. There are several ways this can be done. One method would be to enclose a bathroom scale in a waterproof plastic bag. A second method would be to use a large spring scale to weigh the object while it is submerged. A third method is shown in Figure 4.

Figure 4. Why is less weight required when the object is submerged in the water?

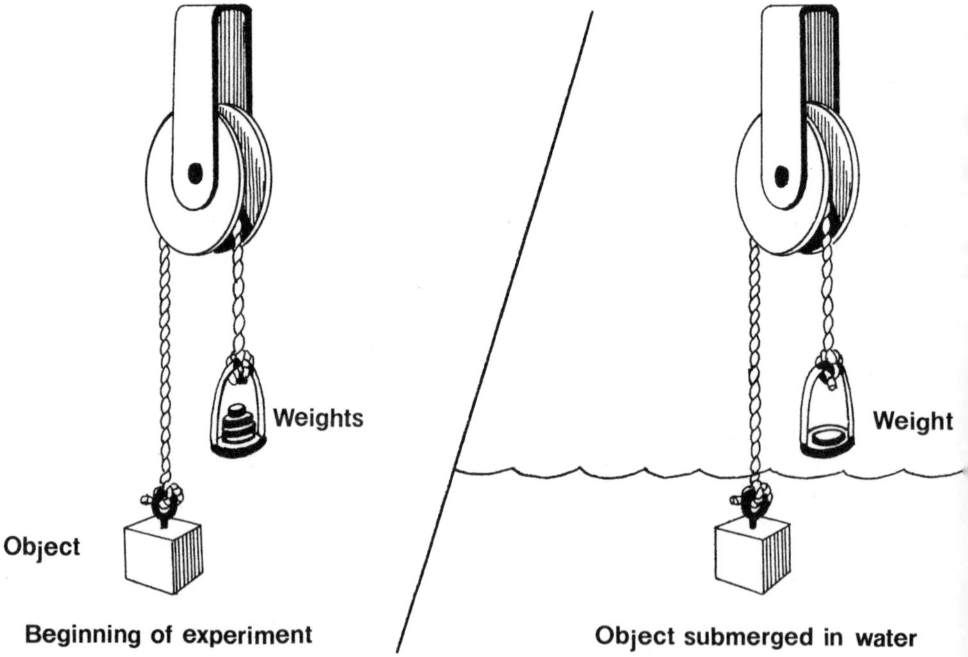

Weights

Object

Beginning of experiment

Weight

Object submerged in water

An object to be weighed is hung on one end of a rope. The rope is run through a pulley and weights are attached on the other end. Heavy metal washers or a bottle of water can be used as weights. The pulley can be held up by a friend or tied to a diving board or tree limb that sticks out over the water. Do you see how this pulley arrangement is like a balance that is used to weigh things? What happens if the weights on the two ends of the rope are not equal?

At the beginning of the investigation, the weight of the object on the left in Figure 4 should be equal to the weight of the objects on the right. Now lower the object on the left into the water. Do you have to add or remove weight from the right side to keep the pulley system balanced?

Perhaps you would like to investigate the amount of weight lost by a submerged object. To do so, measure the amount of water displaced by using a setup similar to that in Figure 2. Use a spring scale or a device as shown in Figure 4 to weigh the object while it is submerged. If you do this carefully, you will see that *the loss of weight of a submerged object is equal to the weight of the water displaced by the object.* Does this sound like a mouthful of words? Think about it for a minute. This is very similar to the statement explaining floating. In the case of a floating object, the loss of weight is equal to the object's own weight; thus the object appears to be weightless in water. If a 10-pound (4.5-kilogram) object displaces 10 pounds of water, it floats. If a 10-pound object displaces only 5 pounds of water, the object does not float. But the object only weighs 5 pounds while submerged in the water.

This loss of apparent weight is very important to scuba divers and others who wish to stay submerged. Since their bodies, air tanks, and other equipment displace water, the buoyant force of the water tends to push them to the surface. What divers usually do is wear a belt made of lead. Their belts often weigh about 20 pounds (9 kilograms) and they help keep the divers submerged.

In summary, remember what you have learned about floating. *An object floats when it displaces its weight in whatever material it is floating in.* A block of wood floating in water displaces an amount of water equal to its weight. A large balloon filled with helium floating in air displaces an amount of air equal in weight to that of the balloon full of helium. A hot-air balloon displaces its weight in the colder air surrounding it; and so on.

HERE'S ONE THAT CAN BE DONE QUICKLY

Not all investigations in the water take as much time as those dealing with floating and buoyancy. There are many you can do in a couple of minutes and perhaps also have some fun puzzling your friends.

Wad up a towel or large cloth and place it in a bucket or other plastic container. A gallon plastic milk container with the top cut off works fine. (Or, if you prefer to do your experiments on a smaller scale, use a handkerchief and a plastic drinking glass.) Turn the bucket upside down. If the towel falls out, a way must be found to keep it in the bucket. One way is to use a small stick a bit longer than the diameter of the bucket.

The stick can be wedged across the inside of the bucket to keep the towel in place.

Holding the bucket mouth downward, lower it into the water in a swimming pool or bathtub until it is completely submerged (see Figure 5). Being careful to keep the bucket mouth downward, remove it from the water. Examine the contents. Why didn't the towel get wet? The answer is that the air keeps the water from entering the bucket.

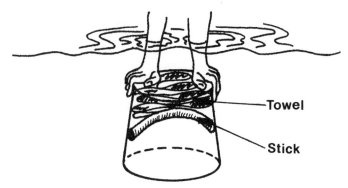

Figure 5. *What keeps the towel from getting wet when the bucket is submerged in the water?*

What happens if the bucket is placed mouth upward into the water? If you let go of the bucket, it probably will tip over and fill with water. What happened to the air that was in the bucket?

To find out, repeat the experiment. This time cover the bucket with a piece of heavy cardboard or a piece of plywood. Slowly remove the cover while the bucket is submerged upright in a foot or so (about 30 centimeters) of water. Bubbles should be enough of a clue for you to figure out what happened to the air.

A bucket of air held mouth downward is much like diving bells used many years ago. Look at the diving bell in Figure 6. What kept the diving bell from turning over and the air escaping?

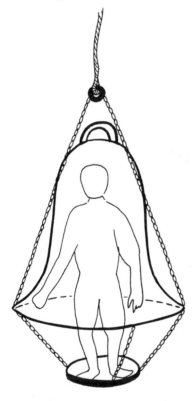

Figure 6. A French scientist proposed this diving bell in the seventeenth century. Do you think it would work?

WHO CAN POUR AIR THE BEST?

As we have already seen, an idea in science sometimes can be used to make up a game. So it is with

26

what we have just learned about the air in buckets held underwater. With this knowledge we can make up a game to be carried on in a pool.

The idea of this game is to see which team of two people can do the best job of pouring air from one container to another underwater.

Each team should use containers of the same size and shape. Small plastic buckets or plastic milk bottles with the tops cut off are ideal. One member of each team swims to the bottom with a container full of air. The other team member stays on the surface and holds a container full of water mouth downward, as shown in Figure 7. The winning team is the one that manages

Figure 7. The idea of this interesting water game is to see who can transfer the most air from the lower container to the upper one.

to transfer the greatest amount of air from the lower to the upper container. This is not as easy as it may seem. One reason is that the buoyancy of the container of air tends to force the lower team member to the surface.

Can you figure out a method of determining which team transferred the greatest amount of air from one container to the other? Hint: It should help if the containers are made of clear plastic.

HOW CAN WE MEASURE THE DEPTH OF WATER?

If you are doing investigations in a swimming pool, perhaps the easiest way to find the depth of the water is to use a long, dry stick. The stick should be lowered vertically until it touches the bottom. Then remove the stick. Use a yardstick or meterstick to measure the length of the part of the stick wet by the water. Or you may wish to lower a weight by means of a dry rope. As in the case of the stick, it is an easy matter to measure the length of the rope wet by the water.

Neither of these methods would be very handy for a diver to use. Fortunately, it is possible to measure the depth of the water using a small device that looks much like a wristwatch, called a depth gauge. The device indicates the depth of the water by measuring the pressure exerted on it.

Place a clear plastic container full of air mouth downward in the water. Notice how the water level inside an inverted container of air moves upward as it is taken into deeper and deeper water. In other words, the volume of air inside the container decreases as it is taken into deeper and deeper water.

28

This decrease in the volume of the air illustrates how the pressure increases with depth. In fact, the pressure increases in direct proportion to the depth of the water. More big words? Not really. All this statement says is that if the depth of the water increases, the pressure also increases.

What happens inside the inverted container also shows how pressure affects air, a gas, differently than it affects water, a liquid. Gases are *compressible*. This means gases can be compressed or their volumes made smaller by applying pressure. The air inside a partly inflated balloon can be compressed into a smaller volume by squeezing the balloon with your hands. In contrast, the volume of liquids is changed very little by the addition of pressure.

All you need to measure water depth using the pressure method is a piece of clear plastic pipe or hose. Or you can cut the bottom of a clear plastic bottle that has straight sides. One end must be closed. If you are using a plastic pipe, a cork will do this nicely.

The inverted pipe full of air is taken into the swimming pool. As you may guess from the results of earlier investigations, the pipe must be held upright with the open end pointing downward. Otherwise the air will escape.

Figure 8 shows what happens to the water level inside the pipe as it is taken into deeper and deeper water. Of course, most swimming pools are not 33 feet (10 meters) deep. Nevertheless, you should be able to detect a small change in the water level inside the tube when it is taken to the deep end of the swimming pool.

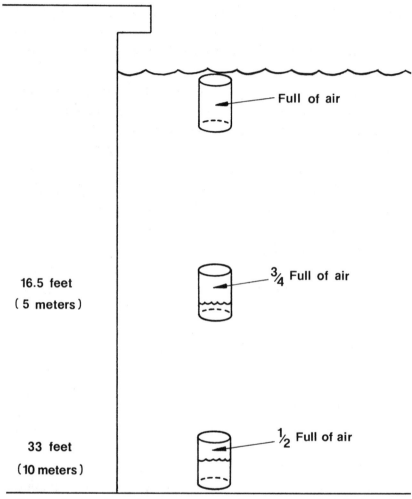

Figure 8. Notice what happens to the amount of air inside the container as it is taken into deeper and deeper water.

The plastic pipe with an open end is not the easiest thing to use underwater. Tip it the least little bit and some of the air escapes. What can be done to make it easier to use?

One thing you might wish to try is covering the open end with a piece of thin rubber (perhaps from a large balloon). Gently stretch the rubber across the tube. Hold it in place with a rubber band as shown in Figure 9.

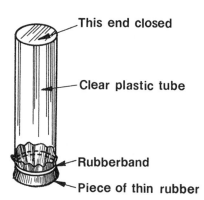

Figure 9. A homemade depth finder.

With rubber covering one end of the tube, the air inside will not be compressed as much as before when it is lowered in the water. Some force will be required to stretch the rubber as well as compress the air inside. You have now made a homemade depth finder. With it you should be able to figure out how the depth finders used by divers work. Do you think there is something inside the wristwatch-like devices that is squeezed by the pressure of the water?

Most barometers, instruments used to measure air pressure, also work on the same principle as your homemade depth gauge. A small box of air inside the barometer slightly changes size as the pressure of the air surrounding the box increases or decreases.

The same is true of altimeters found in airplanes. Those devices are used to measure altitude, or height above the ground. The higher the airplanes go, the less the pressure of the air. As you can see, the science principles involved in your homemade depth gauge have many applications.

THE OLD CAN DEMONSTRATION

There are several ways to demonstrate that the pressure in water varies with the depth of the water. You tried one of these ways when you used the clear plastic tube full of air. The demonstration often shown in science textbooks involves water flowing from holes in the side of a can.

Use as large a container as possible—perhaps an old pail or even a plastic garbage can in which you don't mind having a few holes. That way there will be little doubt about the results. And if you do the demonstration along the side of a swimming pool, you should get results even easier to observe. Besides, there is little chance of water damage if you do your work there instead of inside a building.

Use a hammer and nail to make several holes in the side of the container. One hole should be near the top of the container and another near the bottom. Next fill the container full of water, and keep adding water to keep it full. Observe how the streams of water pour through the holes and strike the surface on which the can rests. Would you have predicted results like those shown on the left side or on the right side of Figure 10?

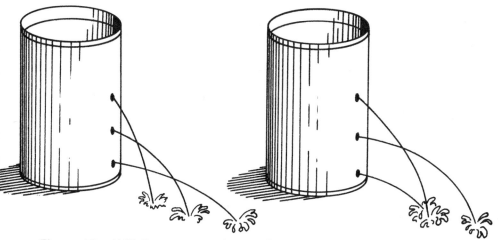

Figure 10. *Will the streams of water flowing from holes in a can form patterns like those shown on the left or those on the right?*

Since the water pressure is greatest at the bottom of the can, you may think the bottom stream will squirt out the farthest. However, when you try it, you will find your results are more like those shown on the right in Figure 10. How can this be? There are two forces acting on each stream of water. The first is a horizontal, or sideways, force resulting from the water pressure in the can. The second is a downward force caused by gravity. The effects of these two forces, however, are not the same.

The horizontal force pushes the water out at a constant rate. In other words, the water travels sideways the same distance the first second of time as the second second, and so on. The force of gravity, however, causes falling objects to speed up as they fall. Thus, the water falls a greater distance the second second than the first. The result is streams of water tracing out patterns like those shown on the right in Figure 10.

What happens if the container is placed on the edge of a swimming pool, or a boat dock, or on a box? Figure 11 shows what happens when each of the streams of water falls a couple of feet or more before striking something. Can you explain these results?

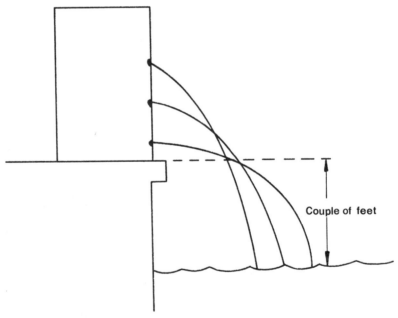

Couple of feet

Figure 11. Is this the result that you get when you try the experiment?

Are you sure that Figure 11 is correct? There is only one really good way to find out. Try it. Doing the investigations is always the best way to make sure something works.

WHO'S THE BIGGEST WINDBAG AROUND THE POOL?

Everybody seems to know that "water seeks its own level." If you pour water in one side of a container, the water runs across the container until it has a level surface.

A way to show this is to use a piece of clear plastic tubing or hose. Hold the tubing in the shape of a "U" as shown in Figure 12. Pour water in one end of the tubing. What happens to the water level on the other side of the "U"?

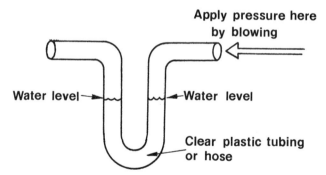

Figure 12.   What happens to the water levels inside the inverted U-tube when pressure is applied to one end?

Now how can we use the inverted U-tube to find out who can blow the hardest? Fill the U-tube so it is about half full of water. Have one person blow in one end as hard as possible. How far can the level of water in the other tube be forced to rise? Who in the crowd around the pool can make the water level rise the farthest? Does this mean that person can blow the hardest?

A manometer is a device that looks like a U-tube and is used to measure pressure. For example, a manometer filled with water is used to measure the pressure in natural-gas lines. Most people are surprised to learn that the pressure of the gas will raise the water level in the manometer only 3 or 4 inches (about 10 centimeters). Of course if the gas was under greater pressure, there would be more chance of a dangerous leak.

WHO SAYS WATER WILL NOT RUN UPHILL?

Most people would agree: Water will not run uphill. In a sense this statement is another example of water seeking its own level. For water to flow uphill, a force has to be applied. To make water rise in one side of the U-tube, you had to blow on the other side. You applied a force.

But there is a way to make water flow uphill without having to apply a force. Or at least it seems that way. Figure 13 shows an easy way to get water out of a bucket. This device is called a siphon.

To set up a siphon, place one end of a hose in a bucketful of water. Place the other end over the side of bucket as in Figure 13. Does the water run up the hose and down over the side of the bucket? It shouldn't. You have to do something to get the siphon started.

Figure 13. Is the water flowing uphill in this siphon?

If you are working with clean water, place your mouth over the end of the hose that hangs alongside the bucket. Suck until the water completely fills the hose. When you remove your mouth, the water should continue to flow.

There also is another way of getting the siphon started. You will want to use this method if you are working with water unsafe to drink.

Place the entire hose in the bucket of water. Move the hose around in such a way that it is completely full of water. Be sure there is no air trapped in the hose. Now place your thumb over one end of the hose so it is completely sealed. Next remove the sealed end of the hose from the bucket and hang it over the side. When you remove your thumb, the water should begin to flow.

In setting up a siphon, you may have discovered an important idea. In order for the water to flow, the end of the hose outside of the bucket must be lower than the water level inside the bucket. If the end of the outside hose is raised higher than the water level in the bucket, the water in the hose runs back into the bucket. Or if the end of the hose inside the bucket comes out of the water, air enters the hose. In either case, we say we have "lost our siphon." In order to get it working again we must use one of the methods described earlier.

It may look like water is flowing uphill in the case of the siphon. But from your investigations you can see that it flows downhill a greater distance than it flows uphill. The siphon works because of differences in pressure caused by the unequal amounts of water in the two ends of the hose.

The action of siphons is important in many ways. Perhaps you have wondered why most communities have laws dealing with the plumbing in houses and other buildings. Of course, it is important that the pipes be installed in such a way as to insure a safe supply of drinking water. The following story shows how the action of a siphon and poor plumbing practices could cause a disaster!

It was early June and all the students at a college had gone home for the summer. In the Biology Building two workers were busy cleaning a laboratory. One job was to clean out the large tank, full of foul-smelling formaldehyde, in which the preserved animals had been stored. All animals had already been removed. First the tank was drained. Once that was done, the plug was placed back in the drain. A hose was connected to a water faucet and the end of the hose placed in the tank. The idea was to fill the tank full of water and to then scrub it out.

At that point one of the workers said to the other, "Let's go eat lunch while the tank is filling."

Everything was fine until the tank was about half full of water. Then suddenly a water main down the street broke. The water pressure all over the campus dropped. The water stopped flowing from faucets, including those in the Biology Building.

But that is not all that happened. The contents of the partially filled tank were pulled back into the city water lines by what plumbers call "back siphoning." This means that, because of siphoning action, the liquid in a pipe moves in a direction opposite that of its usual flow.

You can imagine the reaction of the town's citizens when they found out what was giving their drinking water such a bad taste and smell. And they were convinced of the importance of plumbing being installed so back siphoning could not occur again!

See if you can find out what precautions are taken to prevent back-siphoning from occurring in home plumbing in your community. For example, are hose connections equipped with devices that allow the water to flow in only one direction, as shown in Figure 14? Remove the lid from the top of the flush tank on a toilet. Trace the path of the water from the time it

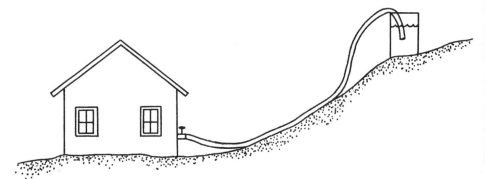

Figure 14.   The faucet on this side of this house is equipped with a device that allows the water to flow in only one direction. Without such a device, what might happen if the water pressure inside the house suddenly dropped?

enters the tank through a supply pipe. Is there any way for the water, once it is in the tank, to get back into the water supply line?

PUTTING IT ALL TOGETHER

Here is an investigation that will allow you to use most of what you have learned about floating objects and pressure. Although the investigation could be done in a swimming pool using giant equipment, it is easier to do on a smaller scale.

Fill a bottle with water. Next fill an eyedropper or small vial about half full of water and place it in the bottle (see Figure 15). Adjust the amount of water in the eyedropper so it just barely floats. Cover the mouth of the bottle with a piece of rubber from a large

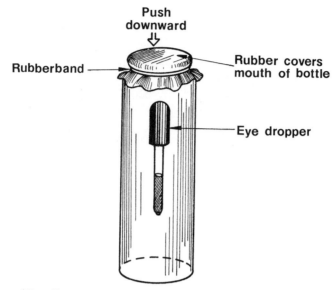

Figure 15. *Be sure to notice what happens to the water level inside the eye dropper when you push down on the rubber covering the mouth of the bottle.*

balloon. Use rubberbands to secure the piece of rubber.

What will happen when you push down on the rubber covering the top of the bottle? Try it. Can you explain what happens to the water level inside the eyedropper?

You may wish to change the apparatus so it looks like the one in Figure 16. The best way to assemble this apparatus is by holding it underwater. When you do so, what happens when you push up on the rubber

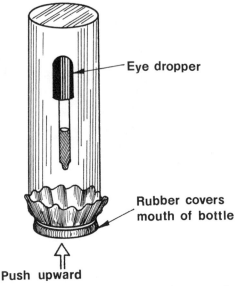

Eye dropper

Rubber covers
mouth of bottle

Push upward

Figure 16.   What happens when you push upward on the rubber covering the mouth of the bottle?

covering the mouth of the bottle? Do you understand what happened?

The apparatus you have been playing with is called a Cartesian diver. How many of the ideas we have investigated so far are involved in explaining how it works?

INVESTIGATING OBJECTS IN MOTION

Perhaps you have seen a cartoon similar to that of the boy in Figure 17. You probably know what happens. As the boy jumps forward, the boat moves backward. Splash! Hope he's a good swimmer!

What happened to the boy and the boat illustrates

Figure 17. What happens when the boy tries to jump from the boat to the dock?

another important science principle: for every action there is an equal but opposite reaction. What does this mean? It means if you push on something, it pushes back with the same amount of force, but in an opposite direction. This is easily shown in the swimming pool.

Lie on a mattress or float so your feet touch the sides of the pool. As you push off with your leg muscles, does the pool move backward as you go forward? Not that you can observe. This suggests we need to change the investigation a bit.

Have a friend lie on another air mattress so your friend's feet touch yours. Your friend's legs should be straight, as shown in Figure 18. Bend your legs so you can give yourself a shove. When you do so, do you move forward? Does your friend move? In what direction? How fast? Does how much you and your friend weigh make a difference? Try the investigation with people of differing weights. Can you explain why, when you shove off from the edge of the pool, the pool doesn't seem to move?

Air mattress

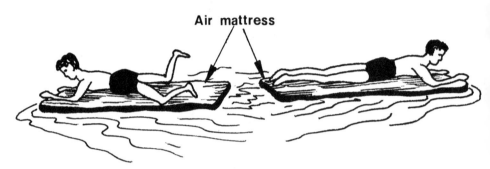

Figure 18. What happens to the boy on the right when the boy on the left uses his legs to shove off?

Figure 19. Why is it necessary to hold the box from which the swimmer is jumping?

44

Can you observe other examples of action and reaction at a swimming pool? For example, why is it necessary for someone to brace the box from which the swimmer is diving in Figure 19?

WHO HITS THE WATER FIRST?

In the introduction to this book, the question was asked about the weight of divers. Does a heavier diver hit the water more quickly than a diver who weighs less? Or in other words, do heavy objects fall faster than lighter objects? The answer is yes if you are comparing a heavy metal ball with a feather or a leaf. We know that air resistance makes a difference—this is why people can safely parachute from an airplane.

But what if the objects are the same size and shape and only differ in weight? This is the question Galileo, the famous Italian scientist, struggled with over 350 years ago. Some people believed he tried to answer the question by dropping objects off the Leaning Tower of Pisa. Others say that this story is not true. Regardless of what you believe about Galileo, you can do your own Leaning Tower of Pisa experiment.

All you need are some objects to drop and a high place to drop them from. If you drop them above water, the splashes will tell you which object falls the fastest. A high diving board, a bridge over a stream, or a high pier on a lake will work fine. For objects you will need something that doesn't cost much. You may not be able to get the objects back if you drop them into a river or lake. Also they should be something that will not pollute the water. Small plastic bottles full of sand or water are one possibility. The sand weighs about five times more than the same volume of water. Another possibility is a steel ball, like a ball bearing, and a wooden or plastic ball the same size. Or if you are dropping the objects into a river or lake, perhaps a round stone and an object of similar size that weighs less. Again, this is an opportunity to improvise.

It is important that the objects be dropped at the same time. Have one person drop both objects, one with each hand. Or push the objects off a diving board, bridge rail, or the dock floor with a stick. The person doing the dropping should be able to see the splashes. However, a person near the surface of the water will be in a better position to decide which object hit the water first.

Which of these two objects does hit the water first? The heavier one or the lighter one? What happens when you repeat the investigation? Do you always get the same results? It is important to do an investigation a number of times to see if you can come up with similar results.

As in the case of many investigations, your results may differ a little from what science books say should happen. Nevertheless, you should be able to show that objects of similar size and shape drop at about the same rate regardless of their weights. So, does the heavier diver reach the water faster than a diver who weighs less? Would you have expected this answer before you did the investigation with falling objects?

While you are investigating falling objects, here is another question you may want to tackle. If one object is dropped and another is thrown horizontally from a bridge or pier, which object hits the water first? Look at Figure 20. Can you design an investigation to answer the question?

Figure 20.   Will the object that is dropped or the object that is thrown hit the water first?

DOES LIGHT ALWAYS TRAVEL IN A STRAIGHT LINE?

When you look at something, you assume that the light reaching your eyes from the object has traveled in a straight line. You see a person standing straight ahead of you. You are certain that you can reach the person by walking toward him. You feel certain of this because you have learned that the light does not bend after it bounces off the person and travels to your eyes. But are you really certain that light always travels in a straight line? Perhaps you have visited the fun house at an amusement park or fair. The light bouncing off the curved mirrors causes all sorts of strange experiences. There also are situations in nature where you may have a hard time believing your own eyes. And many of these situations involve water.

Begin by placing a straight stick about 5 or 6 feet (about 2 meters) long in a swimming pool or other body of clear water. Holding the stick straight up and down with about half of it in the water, as shown on the left in Figure 21, sight or look down the stick. Does it look straight?

Figure 21. Why does the stick look straight when it is placed vertically in the water and appear to be bent when held in the water at an angle?

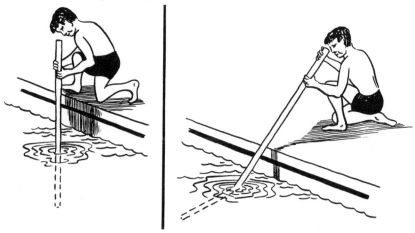

Next place the stick in the water at an angle, as shown on the right in Figure 21. Again sight down the stick. Does it look straight now? How can what you have observed be explained?

The stick appears to be straight when observed in air or when it is held straight up and down in the water. However, when it is held at an angle in the water, it appears bent. This is because light rays are bent when they pass from water to air at an angle. The same is true for light passing from air to water at an angle.

What you have observed is called *refraction*, or the bending of light rays. This is the principle involved in camera and telescope lenses, eyeglasses, and many other optical instruments.

Figure 22 shows another way to demonstrate refraction using water. Shine a bright flashlight into some

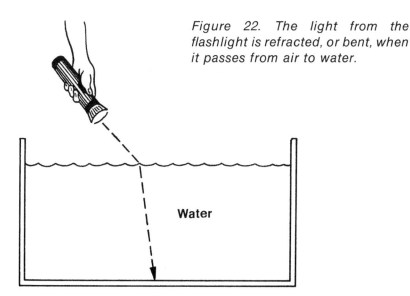

Figure 22. The light from the flashlight is refracted, or bent, when it passes from air to water.

Water

49

clear water at an angle. If it is a dark night and the surface of the water is smooth, you should be able to see how the beam of light is bent.

What would happen if a swimmer near the bottom of the swimming pool would shine a flashlight toward the surface at an angle? Be sure to use a waterproof flashlight or one wrapped in a clear plastic bag if you try this. If you don't want to try this in a swimming pool, use a large aquarium with smooth glass sides. In a dark room you should have no difficulty in seeing what happens when the light beam passes from the water into the air.

People often misjudge the depth of a body of clear water. The water looks as if it is three or maybe four feet deep. They jump in and to their surprise, discover it is over their heads.

Figure 23 shows how the refraction of light can also fool a fisherman. The fish seems closer to the surface

Figure 23. What will happen if the boy shoots the arrow toward the place where the fish seems to be?

Fish seems to be here

Fish is here

than it really is. Be sure to remember this the next time you go fishing—especially if you use a bow and arrow or gig.

IF I CAN'T SEE YOU, HOW CAN YOU SEE ME?

As you have observed, the direction of a beam of light from a flashlight does not change when it shines straight down into the water. When the beam strikes the water at an angle, the beam is refracted or bent. What happens if you keep changing the angle so the beam is striking the water farther and farther away from you? In other words, if the beam of light is almost horizontal, or parallel to the surface of the water?

Try it. It needs to be dark for you to see what is happening. A boat dock on a dark night will be great. Or use the water in a bathtub with the room lights turned off. Or better yet, use a large aquarium. If you add a little flour or powdered milk to the water, you should be able to see the beam of light better.

As you decrease the angle between the light beam and the water's surface, something happens. The light beam is no longer refracted, or bent. Instead the light is *reflected* back into the air, as shown in Figure 24. For light passing from air into water, the angle at which this happens is about 15°. If the angle between the light beam and the water is less than 15°, the light is reflected.

Think about this for a minute. You probably have already observed this phenomenon many times. You look straight down into the clear water and you see the bottom. When you look at the surface of the water some distance away from you, all you see is the light being reflected off its surface.

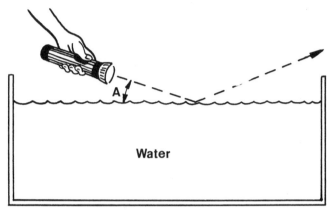

Figure 24. If angle A is less than 15 degrees, the light striking the surface of the water is reflected.

Does this suggest an advantage to having lifeguards sitting in chairs high above the surface of the water? Can they see more of the bottom of the pool than if they were sitting on the edge of the pool? Try it the next time you are at the pool if the lifeguards will give you permission to climb up into one of their chairs.

Figure 25 shows what happens to an underwater beam of light when it strikes the surface. If the angle between the beam of light and the surface of the water is less than $41\frac{1}{2}°$, the light is reflected. Use a waterproof flashlight or one sealed in a clear plastic bag to try this.

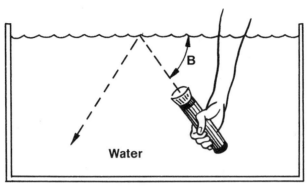

Figure 25. If angle B is less than 41½ degrees, the light striking the surface of the water is reflected.

Now look at Figure 26. Is it possible for the girl on the edge of the pool to see the swimmer and for him not to see her? The answer is yes. Why? Because the

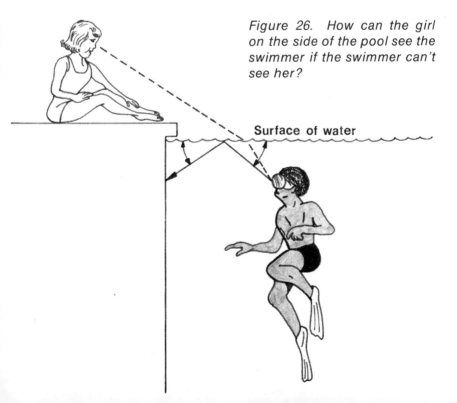

Figure 26. How can the girl on the side of the pool see the swimmer if the swimmer can't see her?

Surface of water

angle at which light is reflected is different if it is going from air to water (15° or less) than if it is going from water to air (41½° or less). Because of reflection, the swimmer sees the side of the pool. Because of refraction, the girl sees the swimmer, but in a slightly different position from where he really is.

Look back at Figure 23. Who has the advantage—the man or the fish? Is it possible for the man to see the fish and for the fish not to see the man? Many fishermen believe it is important to stay as low as possible on a dock or in a boat.

The next time you go swimming, get a friend to help you try out your ideas. Take turns playing the part of the fisherman and the fish. On whose side is science in this case—the fish's or the fisherman's?

What you have learned about how light bounces off and passes through water will be very useful in doing many of the investigations that follow.

Investigating
Science
in Ponds, Lakes,
and Streams

THERE ARE MANY INVESTIGATIONS that can be done
in any size body of water—from the smallest pond or
stream to the largest lake or the ocean. Some of these
investigations are done best from a boat or a dock.
Others can be carried out from the shoreline or in
shallow water. Most involve a study of living things
and factors that affect them.

Safety precautions should always be observed while
working around water. Practice the "buddy system."
This means always work with at least one other
person, and preferably someone who is a good swimmer.

Wear a life preserver when you work from a boat or
near deep water. If you have the opportunity, observe
conservation officials and other government employ-
ees working near the water. They are required to wear
life preservers even though they may be good swimmers.

Boat captains make it a practice to always tell
someone where they are headed before they cast off. It
is also important for you to let someone know where
you will be doing your investigation.

Figure 27 shows some of the things you may wish to

take along. It is also a good idea to wear a pair of old tennis shoes or boots when working near or in the water. Otherwise you may cut your feet on shells or other sharp objects.

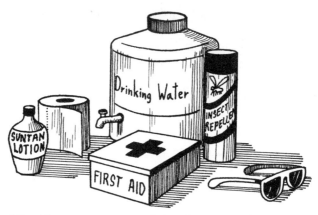

Figure 27. These are some of the things you should take with you on any field trip.

Many investigations require simple equipment that you can easily build and have fun doing so. Let's start with some of this equipment and also find out how it is used.

OBSERVING UNDERWATER

The surface of a body of water acts like a big mirror. Much of the light striking the surface of the water is reflected. This makes it very difficult to observe living things in the water if you are on the surface. One solution, of course, is to get into the water. Perhaps you have seen pictures of living things taken by skin or scuba divers. These beautiful photographs make most of us want to see what is down there.

Besides getting in the water, you can use a seascope to observe living things in a clear body of water. A seascope works much like a glass-bottom boat. It allows you to see what is going on beneath the surface while enjoying the comforts of a rowboat or boat dock.

There are dozens of ways to build a seascope. One way is to use a piece of stovepipe about 7 or 8 inches (18 to 20 centimeters) across and about 24 inches (60 centimeters) long. See Figure 28. It will help if you paint the inside a flat black. This will reduce the amount of light being reflected off the sides of the pipe. One end of the stovepipe must be covered with something that is transparent and which will make the

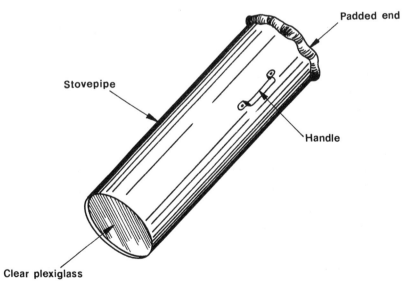

Figure 28. A homemade seascope.

pipe watertight. Try a piece of clear heavy plastic. It can be secured to the pipe with some heavy rubberbands. The other end of the pipe should be wrapped with tape or some other soft material. This will keep the tube from cutting your face and provide for a light-tight seal between the end of the pipe and your face. You may wish to attach handles to the sides of the pipe to make it easier to hold.

You can't afford the price of a piece of stovepipe? No problem: improvise. You can use a piece of heavy cardboard tubing that rugs and other floor coverings come rolled around. Paint will slow down the effects of placing the cardboard tubing into the water. Or you may wish to make a seascope by building a wooden box out of plywood. It should be about 30 inches (75 centimeters) long and about 6 inches by 6 inches (15 centimeters) square where you place your face. The end that goes in the water is made of clear Plexiglas and is glued in place.

When the seascope is used, there is no advantage to submerging it more than a couple of inches (5 centimeters). See Figure 29. Since the water pressure increases with depth, placing it too far into the water may cause it to leak.

Your homemade seascope can be used anytime you wish to observe living things in the water. Perhaps you want to know if there are any fish around the posts holding up a boat dock. Or you are interested in collecting shells from deep water. If you could only see the shells, you could bring them to the surface with a scoop attached to the end of a long pole.

Figure 29. *A seascope can be used from a boat or dock to observe living things in lakes and other bodies of water.*

THE SECCHI DISK

Sometimes the water is not very clear. As a result you may have difficulty seeing very far beneath the surface. In doing their investigations scientists often need to measure the clearness of the water. One of the pieces of equipment they use is the Secchi disk, which is simple to make and easy to use. The hardest part is pronouncing its name (sek-ee).

Cut a circle 8 inches (20 centimeters) in diameter from a piece of stiff metal or plywood. Drill a $^3/_8$-inch (.95-centimeter) hole in the center. Use a ruler to divide the disk into four quarters. Paint two of the opposite quarters white. Paint the other two quarters black, as shown in Figure 30. Use two nuts to attach an eyebolt to the circle as also shown in Figure 30. If the disk has been made of a material that floats, it will be necessary to attach some weights to the lower side.

Fasten a rope to the eyebolt. Since the rope will be

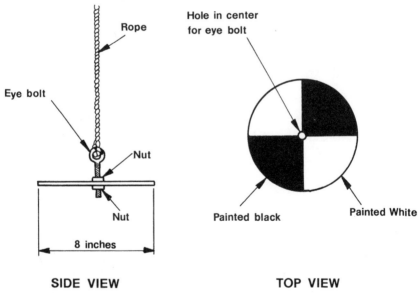

SIDE VIEW   TOP VIEW

Figure 30.   The Secchi disc is used to measure the clearness of the water.

used to lower the disk into the water, it should be a type not damaged by water. Place knots in the rope at one foot intervals.

To determine the clearness of the water, slowly lower the Secchi disk into the water. Keep track of the number of knots in the rope that are submerged. This will tell you the depth of the Secchi disk when it is no longer visible. This depth may vary from a few inches in a muddy river to more than 100 feet (30 meters) in a clear mountain lake.

The depth at which the Secchi disk can no longer be seen from the surface tells us the approximate depth to which light is penetrating the water. This is very important to know. Without light, green plants cannot produce food. If the Secchi disk can be seen only in the top 6 feet (2 meters) of a pond or lake, then we know that this is where all the food making by green plants is taking place. Since many animals feed on these green plants, it also indicates that many of them will be found in this upper layer of water.

You can use the Secchi disk to investigate many questions. Here are just a few:

1. What is the difference in the depth at which a Secchi disk can be seen in a body of water before and after a rain?

2. How does the clearness of the water in a pond, lake, or stream vary during the course of a year?

3. Is the water clearer above or below a dam?

4. In the case of salt water, what effect does the tide have on the distance you can see the disk?

Now here's how measurements made with the Secchi disk can be used to investigate living things.

COLLECTING PLANKTON

Plankton is a term used to describe all the microscopic plants and animals found in water. These organisms are important because they are the source of food for many of the larger animals. We can also find out some things about the conditions in a body of water by examining the plankton it contains.

A plankton net is used to collect these tiny organisms. Materials needed to build a plankton net include: a wide-mouth plastic bottle with a tightly fitting cap; a wire coat hanger or other stiff piece of wire; a needle and heavy thread; an old nylon hose; 20 to 30 feet (7 to 10 meters) of heavy cord or rope.

Bend the coat hanger into a circle (use a wire cutter to remove the hook part of the coat hanger). The top of the hose is then stretched over the wire circle. If you are using an old panty hose, just use one leg. Use a needle and heavy thread to fasten the hose to the wire frame.

Cut the foot off the bottom of the stocking hose. Also cut a large hole in the top of the cap. Be sure to leave enough of the cap so it still can be screwed on the bottle. Insert the bottom of the hose through the hole in the cap and over the mouth of the bottle. This way, when you screw the cap on, the hose will be securely fastened to the bottle as shown in Figures 31 and 32.

Make a bridle by attaching four short pieces of cord to the wire frame. Tie these four cords together and attach a long cord or tow rope as shown in Figure 31.

Throw the net into a pond, lake, or stream and pull it back toward the shore about ten times. Or you can pull the plankton net alongside a dock, or tow it from a

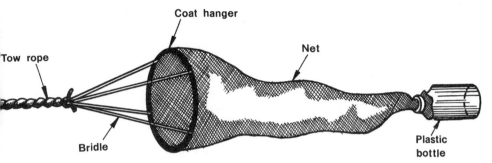

Figure 31. A plankton net.

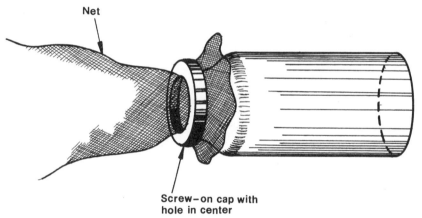

Figure 32. Close-up view showing how the bottle is attached to the plankton net.

boat. Try not to spill the contents of the bottle as you do this. The open end of the net acts as a funnel to trap the organisms in the water. The net concentrates the plankton because more water is pulled through the net than ends up in the bottle.

Remove the bottle from the net by unscrewing the cap. Examine its contents. Although you may be able to see some organisms with the naked eye or a magnifying glass, a microscope will be of great help. If you don't have a microscope, perhaps you can borrow one from a friend or use one in a school laboratory. Figure 33 shows some of the organisms you may find in a plankton sample taken from a pond or lake.

As we have seen, a Secchi disk is used to measure the clearness of the water in a pond or lake. This

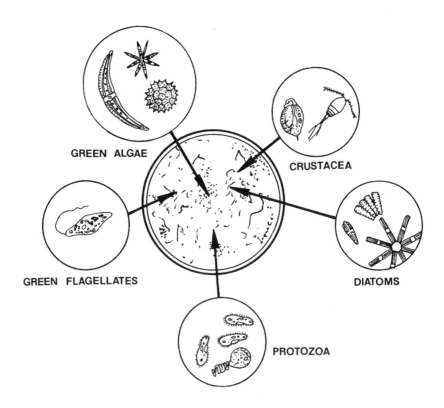

GREEN ALGAE

CRUSTACEA

GREEN FLAGELLATES

DIATOMS

PROTOZOA

VIEW THROUGH MICROSCOPE

Figure 33. Some of the organisms making up plankton in a pond or lake.

measurement tells us how far the light is penetrating. What is the relationship between the depth of light penetration and the amount of plankton found at various depths? All you need to investigate this question is a Secchi disk, a plankton net, and a microscope.

Try collecting plankton at various depths. You may have to tie weights on the net and adjust the speed at which you pull it in order to get deep-water samples.

Perhaps you are more interested in the larger animals in the water. If so, the next investigation will help you with ways to collect these animals.

CAPTURING ANIMALS THAT LIVE IN THE WATER

A dip net is a handy piece of equipment for collecting small fish, tadpoles, water insects, and the hundreds of other kinds of animals that live along the shore and in shallow streams. The materials needed to build a dip net include: an old broomstick for a handle; about 4 feet (120 centimeters) of heavy wire or small metal rod that can be bent; material with which to make the net; heavy thread and a needle; a hose clamp that will fit over the handle.

Figure 34 shows how the dip net will look when it is finished. The first step is to make a metal hoop about 12 inches (30 centimeters) across, as shown in Figure 35. The two ends of the hoop, which are attached to the handle, should be about 4 inches (10 centimeters) long and 1 inch (2 to 3 centimeters) apart. The easiest way to shape the hoop is to bend the metal around a wastebasket or other round container that is about a foot in diameter.

Next chisel or carve two grooves on opposite sides of

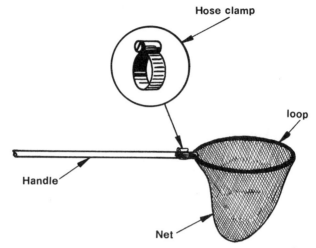

Figure 34. *A dip net is easy to make and very useful in collecting animals that live in shallow water.*

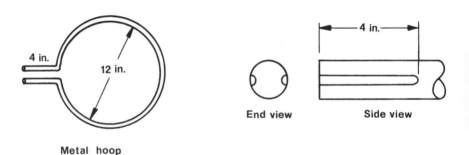

Figure 35. *Parts used in making a dip net.*

one end of the wooden handle. The ends of the metal hoop should fit into these grooves. Slip a hose clamp, which you should be able to buy at a filling station or hardware store, over the end of the handle. Use a screwdriver to tighten the hose clamp so that the metal hoop is securely fastened to the wooden handle.

66

There are many different materials that can be used to make the net—mosquito netting, cheesecloth, the end of a nylon laundry bag, etc. The water will pass more easily through a net that has larger spaces in the fabric. But so will the smaller organisms. Because of this you may wish to make nets of differing materials to use for different purposes. Use a needle and thread to sew the net to the metal hoop.

Be sure you are familar with the fish and other wildlife laws in your state before you start collecting. Also do not take specimens you don't need or don't plan to use in future investigations. If your only interest is to find out what lives in a body of water, return the organisms to the water as soon as you have recorded your data.

There are many questions that can be investigated using a dip net. What lives in the shallow water along the shoreline of the body of water you are studying? Does this vary with the time of day or year? What lives in the grass and other vegetation that covers the banks? Don't overlook flying insects that can be collected with a dip net.

A seine is a type of net used to collect fish and other large animals. If you don't have one, a piece of netting or screen wire attached to two long sticks can serve as a substitute. See Figure 36. The netting or screen wire should be at least 5 or 6 feet (2 meters) long and 3 feet (1 meter) high. The longer the seine, the better. A longer seine allows you to cover more area and there is less chance for the animals to swim around one end of it.

It takes two people to use a seine. Carry the seine

into water about waist deep. Lower it so the sticks touch the bottom. Very slowly move toward the shore. Hold the sticks at a slight angle, with the bottom of the sticks pointing shoreward. This will help keep the lower edge of the seine on the bottom; otherwise, many of the animals in the water will escape under the net.

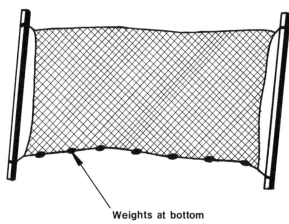

Weights at bottom

Figure 36. Netting or screen wire attached to two sticks can be used as a siene to capture animals living in shallow water along the shore.

As you reach the edge of the water, carefully pull the net up on the shore. Observe what you have captured and then return the organisms you don't want to the water while they are still alive.

A seine doesn't work well in places that have a rocky bottom. The seine catches on the rocks and it often is necessary to lift the seine in order to get it free. When you do this, many of the trapped animals escape. If you are working in a shallow stream with a rocky bottom, hold the seine across the stream and let the water flow through it. Use your hands or a dip net to remove the organisms as they are washed against the seine. You may wish to have a friend go upstream and disturb the bottom with a stick. Animals hiding under the rocks then can be captured downstream in your seine.

How can fish and other animals that live in deep water be captured? If it is fish you are after, you can always try a fishhook baited with a worm. But perhaps a better way is to use a trap, if it is legal to do so where you are working.

Most traps used to catch fish, lobsters, crabs, and other marine organisms operate on the same principle. There are several openings in the sides or ends of the trap. See Figure 37. Attached to each opening is a funnel with the small end pointing inward. An animal entering the trap moves from the larger end of the funnel to the hole at the small end. Once inside, the animal cannot find its way back out.

You can build a trap using screen wire, chicken wire, or similar materials. What you should use will depend in part on what you are trying to catch. You may wish to check with local fishermen for ideas on what to use and how to design your trap. Some traps are made by covering a wooden frame with some type of wire fabric. Others are made by rolling the wire fabric in the form of a cylinder and attaching funnel entrances to each end. In designing your traps, be sure to provide a way to remove any animals you catch. A door in the side works fine.

Traps made partly of wood can be held on the

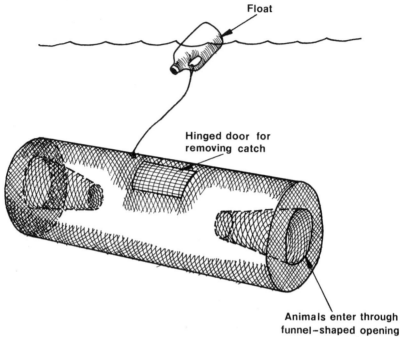

Figure 37.   Traps like this one are used to catch fish and other animals that live in the water.

bottom by placing a few large rocks inside. Tie one end of a heavy cord to the trap and the other end to an empty plastic milk jug. The lid should be tightly screwed on the jug. The jug serves as a float to mark the place where your trap is placed. The cord is used to bring the trap to the surface when you want to find out what you have caught.   To catch certain kinds of animals, traps must be baited. For example, many people use uncooked chicken necks and backs to catch crabs found in many waters along the seashore. Again,

70

check with local fishermen for ideas on what to use for bait.

WHAT'S ON THE BOTTOM?

If you are working in shallow water, you can use a simple dredge like the one shown in Figure 38 to collect bottom samples. It is made by bolting a large coffee can to a long stick or pole. Use a hammer and large nail to punch several holes in the bottom so the water can flow through.

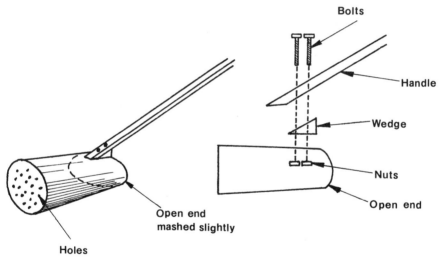

Figure 38. A dredge for collecting samples from the bottom of a pond or lake can be made by fastening a long handle to a large metal can.

Pull the can across the bottom with a motion like one you would use to rake leaves. Place what you collect in pans or pails for later study. Be sure to label

71

each sample so you will know when and where you took it. For example, a piece of paper taped to a pail might read "Sample #9: 9:30 A.M., June 21, 1978 Adams Creek, just below Highway 42 bridge."

The dredge can be modified for use in deep water. A bridle and towrope is attached to the open end of a large can in the same way the plankton net was rigged. A heavy weight attached to the end of the can will keep it on the bottom as it is pulled along. A deep-water dredge also can be made using a rectangular can, such as wax and many cleaners come in. This will give a straight edge that will dig into the bottom.

The material dredged from the bottom can be studied many ways. Run some of it through screens of various sizes. These can be made by tacking screen wire or pieces of cloth to wooden frames.

What living things are present? Is the bottom mainly mud, sand, or rock? How does the material dredged from the bottom vary from one location to another?

COLLECTING WATER SAMPLES

Many scientific investigations require that water samples be taken at various depths in a body of water. It is easy to build your own equipment to do this. Tie a heavy cord around a glass or plastic bottle as shown in Figure 39. A glass bottle has the advantage of allowing you to see what is inside. A plastic one won't break.

A rock or other heavy weight is tied to the bottom. Otherwise, the bottle will float when it is sealed full of air. Also, the weight keeps the mouth of the bottle upward so it will fill with water when the rubber stopper or cork is removed. Notice how, in Figure 39,

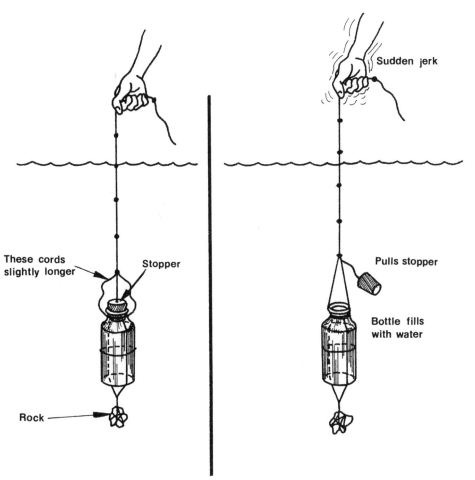

Figure 39. This equipment is used to collect water samples from various depths.

the cord holding the bottle branches is tied to the harness surrounding the bottle. The cord tied to the stopper is slightly shorter than the other two pieces.

The bottle is lowered to the depth from which you wish to collect a sample of water. Knots tied at regular intervals in the cord are a big help in getting the bottle to the desired depth. The cord is then given a quick jerk. This removes the stopper and the bottle fills with water. The bottle is then raised to the surface for observation.

There are many things you can do with the samples of water you collect. If you have a microscope, examine each sample for microscopic organisms. The acid condition of the water can be determined using test paper (called pH paper) that can be obtained in many drugstores or places that sell chemicals. Or the acid condition of the water can be found by using the sets of liquids people use for testing the water in their swimming pools.

HOW COLD IS IT DOWN THERE?

Scientists often want to know the temperature of the water at various depths. So do fishermen. Anyone who has fished knows that fish often are caught in different places in the summer and in the spring. In the spring they may be in the shallow water near the shore of a pond or lake. Summer finds them in the deeper water.

The explanation given for this is that the fish go into deeper water in the summer because it is cooler than the shallow water. Is this really true? How does the water temperature vary in different parts of a pond or lake? Is the water temperature the same near the surface as near the bottom? These are just samples of the questions involving water temperature you can have fun investigating.

Scientists and many fishermen have special thermometers with which to measure the temperatures at various depths. An ordinary thermometer can be used. However, we will have to make one change in how we use it.

Usually we put the thermometer into the substance whose temperature we wish to measure. Then we read the thermometer. But this won't work if we want to measure the temperature at the bottom of the lake. By the time we could pull it back up, the temperature indicated by the thermometer may have changed.

The easiest way to find out the temperature of the water at various depths is to use the water sampling bottle described earlier. A sample of water is taken at a certain depth and brought to the surface. The thermometer is then placed in the bottle and the temperature of the water taken. Since water heats up and cools off slowly compared to air, the temperature of the water sample will change very little in the minute or so that it will take you to do this.

A few questions about water temperatures have already been suggested. Once you get going, you should be able to ask additional ones. Don't overlook the possibilities in the wintertime. If a pond or lake is frozen over, what is the temperature of the water under the ice? *Caution:* Do not go out on the ice unless the proper officals have indicated it is safe to do so. And then you should practice the buddy system.

The next investigation is one you can do inside on a rainy day. What you learn by doing the investigation will be helpful in explaining some of the things you may observe about temperatures in a body of water.

INVESTIGATING A STRANGE PROPERTY OF WATER

What is the relationship between the temperature of water and its volume? If a pond is completely full of cold water, what will happen when the sun warms the water? What will happen to the volume of the water if the weather turns cold? To the volume of the water if it freezes? As in the case of a few other investigations in this book, this one is easier to do first on a small scale. Once we have described the scientific principles involved, we can apply what we have learned to ponds, lakes, and even oceans.

What may seem like a strange property of water can be investigated using a glass bottle, a clear plastic soda straw, a cork, and a thermometer. Or better yet, use a piece of glass tubing instead of the plastic soda straw—the smaller the inside diameter of the straw or tubing, the better.

Assemble the apparatus as shown in Figure 40. The hole in the cork should be just large enough for the straw or tubing to pass through.

Place a drop of liquid soap or some water on the end of the glass tubing. This will make the glass tubing go through the cork more easily. Wrap the glass tubing in a towel and also hold the cork with a towel. Then *gently* push the tubing through the cork with a twisting motion.

Notice in Figure 41 that your hands should be placed close together. This reduces the chance of breaking the glass tubing. Do not hold the tubing or the cork so that an end of the tubing is pointing toward or pushing against the palm of your hand. If the tubing should break, you don't want it to ram into you hand.

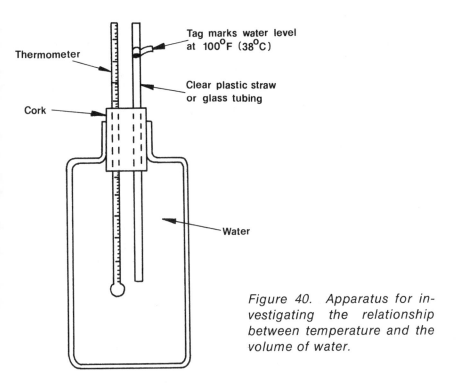

Figure 40. Apparatus for investigating the relationship between temperature and the volume of water.

Figure 41. The glass tubing and rubber stopper should be held in such a way that an injury will not result if the tubing should break.

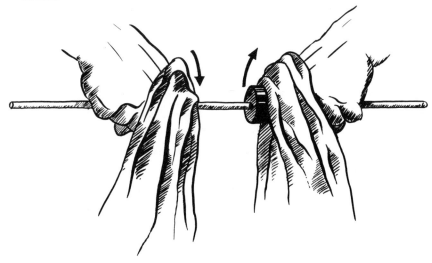

You can use this same procedure to insert a thermometer into a cork.

If you have a thermometer, it should be inserted through a second hole in the cork or placed inside the container. Since the apparatus must be watertight, you may need to place a drop or two of glue or sealing wax around the tubing and the thermometer next to the cork.

Fill the bottle full of water that is at a temperature of about 100°F (38°C). Insert the cork, with the tubing and the thermometer attached, into the bottle. Ideally the water level inside the tubing should be between two-thirds and three-fourths of the way to the top. You may need to remove the cork and either add water or pour water out of the bottle until the water level in the tubing is where you want it. There should be no air in the bottle.

While the water inside the bottle is still near 100°F, mark the level of the water in the tubing. This can be done by wrapping a small piece of Scotch tape around the tube. The bottom of the tape should be level with the top of the water inside the tube. If you wish, you can attach a small piece of paper to the tape and mark the temperature on it.

Place the bottle in a large container of water and ice, as shown in Figure 42. As the water inside the bottle cools, you should be able to detect the water level falling inside the tubing. This is because water, like most materials, *contracts* (its volume gets smaller) when cooled.

If you carefully observe the water level in the tube, you may be able to detect the lowest point it reaches.

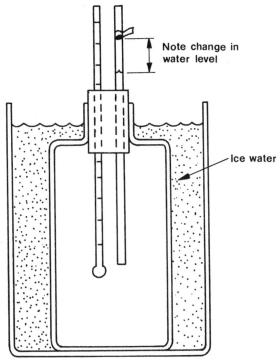

Figure 42.   By placing the apparatus in a container of ice water, you should be able to detect a change in the water level in the glass tubing.

As the temperature of the water in the bottle approaches the freezing point of water (32°F or 0°C), the water begins to expand. It will help if you add some table salt to the ice-water bath and stir it. This will lower the temperature of the solution surrounding the bottle and speed up the cooling of the water inside the bottle.

You probably will not be able to detect the exact temperature at which the water inside the bottle begins to expand. Scientists have found this temperature to be 39°F (4°C). If water at 39°F is either heated *or* cooled, the water expands. This may seem like a strange property; it certainly results in some interesting phenomena involving water. Why does ice float? What is the temperature of the water at the bottom of an ice-covered lake? Why doesn't a lake freeze from the bottom up? These are just a few of the questions you may wish to tackle with your new knowledge of the way water expands and contracts. And if that isn't enough, why did the temperature of the ice and water decrease when the table salt was added?

THERE ARE MANY OTHER INVESTIGATIONS YOU CAN DO WHILE NEAR THE WATER

Not all the observations you make, and the investigations you can do on a pond or lake, are directly related to water. Many depend more on your being out-of-doors. Some of these also work best when you are away from the noise of the city. Others require a dark night, which is never possible where there are lots of lights. People vacationing on a lake or at the seashore often are in a good spot to really hear and see nature. Here is an example of something you may wish to try.

One day you are on a lake fishing and you see a man repairing his boat dock. The man hits a nail with a hammer. He pulls his arm back to strike another blow. When his arm is all the way back, you hear the "bang."

You see the man as the result of light being reflected off him. The light that reaches your eyes travels at a speed of 186,000 miles (300,000 kilometers) per second. But the speed of sound is another matter. Sound travels at the rate of about 1,130 feet (334 meters) per second. In other words, it takes sound about 5 seconds to travel a mile (3 seconds to travel a kilometer). Because of the rapid speed of light, you see the man strike the nail almost at the same instant he does it. Because sound travels at a slower rate, you hear the blow later.

You can use this information in making observations and in doing investigations. If you measure the time between when you see a sound produced and when you hear it, you can estimate the distance you are from the source of the sound. For example, if you see the smoke from a boat engine being started and hear the sound about 3 seconds later, the boat is about 3,400 feet (1,000 meters) away. If you see lightning and then hear the thunder 5 seconds later, you know it was about a mile, or 5,500 feet (1.6 kilometers), away.

You can check this out by measuring the length of time it takes sound to travel a known distance. For example, have a friend about 3,400 feet (1,000 meters) away make a loud sound, by banging on a metal object or beating on a drum. Since sound travels better across water, it will help if you can do this on a lake. Time how long it takes for the sound to reach your ear. If you don't have a watch with a second hand, count silently, "one thousand and one, one thousand and two," and so on. It takes most people about a second to say "one thousand and one." With your friend 3,400 feet away, it should take the sound about 3 seconds to reach you.

Sound travels faster through cold air than through warm air. The speed of sound at 68°F (20°C) is 1,130 feet (334 meters) per second. For each degree Fahrenheit of change in temperature, the speed of sound changes about 1 foot per second. In metric units, this figures out to be about 0.5 meters per second for each degree Celsius of change in temperature. This means that the speed of sound is more than 1,160 feet per second when the temperature is 32°F. At 100°F, sound travels at about 1,100 feet per second.

Sound travels through many materials at a faster rate than it does through air. For example, sound travels through steel at the rate of 16,400 feet (5,000 meters) per second. Perhaps you have seen a Western movie where one of the actors jumped off his horse and put his ear to a railroad track. Do you think he could hear the sound of the approaching train sooner through the steel rail than through the air?

Sound travels through water at the rate of about 4,700 feet (1,400 meters) per second. If a loud noise occurs on the surface of the water, can it be heard faster through the air or faster through the water? Can you devise an investigation to test your ideas?

Stay alert for questions to investigate on ponds, lakes, and streams. Also, if all your own investigations must be done on an inland body of water, see how many of the following beach investigations you can modify and do on a lake.

Investigations at the Beach

SPENDING A VACATION at the beach can be great fun. There are thousands of things to do—swimming, fishing, kite flying, beachcombing, exploring, and just plain relaxing. And what is more relaxing than leaning back in a beach chair and watching the waves come in? Or standing in the surf and letting waves break against your body? Or lying on a surfboard or rubber raft on a calm day and letting the waves gently raise and lower your floating bed?

STUDYING WAVES

If you stand in an ocean surf or in the water along the shoreline of a large lake, the incoming waves may be strong enough to knock you over. Or if you throw a beach ball or some other object that floats into the water, the breaking surf will soon bring it back to the shore. However, a boat or other object floating out beyond where the surf is breaking peacefully bobs up and down.

Why do floating objects behave the way they do? Outside of where the waves are breaking, they bob up and down—but they move very little in any other direction. In where the waves are breaking along the shoreline, the force of the waves sends floating objects crashing toward the beach. Often they are also carried parallel to the beach as they are moved shoreward. To explain why these things happen, we need to do some investigations dealing with waves on water.

If you drop a pebble into a smooth body of water, you will notice that the waves go out in all directions. If there is a stick floating in the water, is it carried along by the waves? The answer is no. The stick bobs up and down as the waves pass. However, the stick moves very little in the direction the waves are moving.

You may wish to test the effect of waves on a floating object. Place a floating object in a body of water on which there are waves. A piece of lumber painted a bright color works nicely. The bright color will help you keep track of the object. The floating object should not stick out of the water very much. Since the wind is usually blowing in the direction the waves are traveling, a high floating object such as a beach ball will be moved by the wind blowing against it.

If you are doing your investigation where there is a surf, you must place the floating object beyond where the waves are breaking. Wade out as far as is safe and then throw the object out beyond the breakers. Or perhaps you can drop the object off a fishing pier or from a boat. Does the floating object move shoreward at the same rate that the waves do?

The effect of waves on a floating object can also be investigated in a large tub or a wading pool. In fact, you can make a game out of it. Place a small cork or other object that floats in the middle of the container.

The water should be at least 1 foot (30 centimeters) deep.

The idea of the game is to see who can move the object to the side of the container by dropping small stones or marbles in the water, as shown in Figure 43.

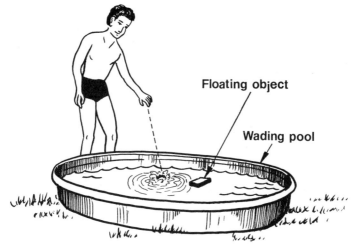

Floating object

Wading pool

Figure 43. Can stones be dropped in such a way that the waves produced make the floating object move across the water?

You may wish to mark spots on the sides of the container as home base for each player. To win the game, you have to drop the stones so that the waves produced move the cork to your home base. After a stone is dropped, you should allow the water to get calm before the next person drops a stone. Since the cork will be moved across the water very little by the waves, you will have to put on a "thinking cap" to win the game. Once you have an idea, try it. For example, does dropping a stone so it strikes the water very close

85

to the cork make the cork move across the water more than when the stone strikes the water farther from the cork?

SCIENTISTS STUDY WAVES IN THE LABORATORY

Scientists build large wave tanks to study the motion of waves on water. Wave tanks are often several feet across and 4 or 5 feet (about 1.5 meters) deep. Some tanks are more than 50 feet (15 meters) long. The sides of the tanks are made of glass or some other transparent material. This allows the scientist to observe what happens to small particles in the water when waves move across the surface.

Waves in a wave tank can be produced by a big paddle at one end that moves back and forth. Or the waves can be generated by a big fan moving air across the surface of the water. Wind is a major cause of waves on lakes and the ocean.

Figure 44 shows how the waves look when viewed through the side of a wave tank. The *crest* is the highest part of the wave and the *trough* is the lowest part. Waves can be measured for both length and height. As shown in Figure 44, the horizontal distance

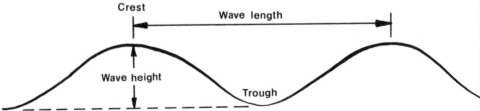

Figure 44. *The time for two successive waves to pass a point is called the* wave *period.*

between wave crests is called the *wave length.* The wave length is also equal to the distance from trough to trough. The vertical distance between the crest and trough is called the *wave height.*

Waves are timed by measuring the time it takes for two waves to pass a spot. This length of time is called a *wave period.* A little later, we will see how some of these wave characteristics can be measured in the ocean or on a lake.

Scientists also use a wave tank to investigate why floating objects are not moved horizontally by waves. They place particles in the water that are neutrally buoyant. This means that the density of the particles is such that they neither sink nor go to the surface, but float below the surface. The presence of these particles in the water allows observers to detect movement in the water.

Figure 45 shows what happens to the particles in the water when the wave passes. The particles trace out a

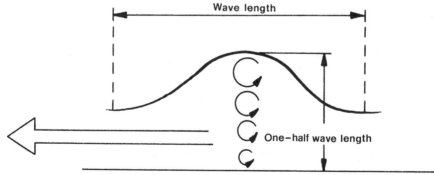

Figure 45. Notice how the particles trace out circles as the wave passes and how the wave distributes only the water to a depth equal to one-half of the wave length.

series of circular patterns. These patterns correspond to the movement of the water as the wave passes. They disturb the water to a depth of one-half the wave length. If the waves are 30 feet (10 meters) apart, the effects of the wave can be felt to a depth of 15 feet (5 meters). Below that depth, a diver would not be disturbed by the waves passing overhead.

An object floating on the water in a wave tank bobs up and down as the wave passes. It also is carried back and forth a bit. However, the object does not move the length of the wave tank with the wave. This explains why a swimmer resting on an air mattress may remain in the same spot as the wave passes him by.

If you are doing your investigations in the water where submerged plants are growing, you can easily observe the effects of passing waves on objects below the surface. Compare the seaweed in Figure 46 with the particles in Figure 45. Notice how the upper parts of the seaweed move toward the wave as the crest approaches. Notice also how it continues to point

Figure 46. The motion of the seaweed produces a clue to how the water particles move as the wave passes.

toward the wave until the crest of the next wave draws near. Do you see how the movements of these plants correspond to the way the particles move in Figure 45?

If you observe enough waves pass in a wave tank, you will notice that there is a slight movement of some of the particles in the direction the waves are moving. This slow shift is called *mass movement* or *mass transport.* Although this movement of water is important to an oceanographer, we can ignore it in most of our investigations.

MEASURING WAVE CHARACTERISTICS

It is important to know as much as possible about the waves striking a shoreline if you plan to study what is happening there. How high are the waves? What is the wave period? At what angle do they strike the shore? What are the effects of waves striking a shoreline at an angle other than 90°?

Finding the wave period is easy if the waves aren't too high. Stand in the shallow water along the shoreline and record the time (to the nearest second) when a wave strikes you. Count off the next nine waves that strike you. When the tenth wave passes by, again record the time. The difference between the two times you recorded, divided by nine, represents the average time between each wave. (Why *nine* when we counted off ten waves? Make ten marks across a sheet of paper. How many spaces are there between the marks?)

What if the waves are too high or you can't get into the water? Perhaps you can make your measurements by observing the waves as they strike the posts under a pier or dock. Or you can use a fishing rod and reel to throw a large float out into the water. You then can stand on the shore and watch the float go up and down as each wave passes. You should be able to get a fairly accurate measurement of wave period using either of these methods.

If the waves aren't too high you can measure wave height with a yardstick or meterstick. A longer stick, two or three yards or meters long, marked off in inches or centimeters, will work even better. Stand in the water with one end touching the bottom. First note the water level on the measuring stick when the trough or low part of the wave passes. Next note the water level when the high part or the crest of the wave strikes the measuring stick. The difference between the two readings is the wave height. With a little practice you should be able to get good results.

If the waves are too high to measure with a measuring stick, you can estimate their height by watching them strike a post or piling in the water. Even scientists with elaborate equipment have difficulty in measuring the height of large waves. This is especially true at sea. How can the height of a wave be accurately measured from a ship which itself is being carried up and down by the motion of the water?

To determine the angle at which the waves are striking the beach, use a stick to make a line in the sand that is parallel to the edge of the water (see Figure 47). Next make a line on the beach that is parallel to the wave crests offshore. If you stand on a dune or some other high structure you should be able to make a more accurate estimate of this direction.

The two lines on the beach should be made long

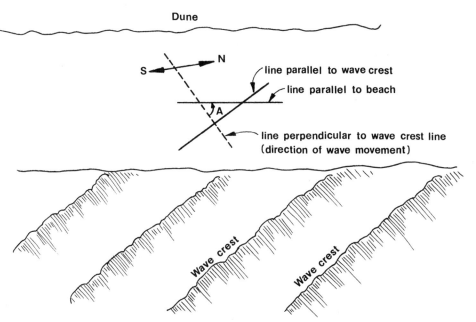

Figure 47. By marking lines on the beach, it is possible to determine the angle at which the waves are striking the beach.

enough so they cross as do those in Figure 47. Next make a line on the beach that is perpendicular to the wave crest line. This is the direction of the wave movement. Angle A in Figure 47 is the angle at which the waves are striking the beach. You can use a protractor to measure the size of this angle on the beach you are studying.

What if you want to know the direction of the wave movement? This is easy to find by drawing another line on the beach that points north. If you don't know your directions, use a magnetic compass to find north. Or observe the direction of the shadow cast by a stick at noon. Or you can find north at night by noting the position of the North Star. Figure 48 shows how you can use the two pointer stars in the Big Dipper to help you find the North Star. Studying the stars provides more interesting activities that can be done at the beach.

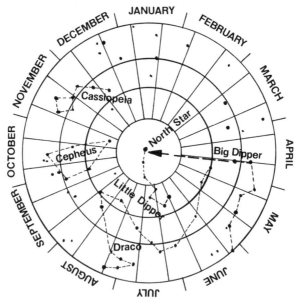

Figure 48. *If you turn this map so the present month is on the top, the map shows the positions of the Big Dipper and other stars in the Northern Sky at 9:00 p.m. Standard Time. Notice how the two stars in the Big Dipper point toward the North Star.*

In Figure 47 the dotted line representing the direction of wave movement crosses the north-south line at an angle of about 75°. Thus we say that the waves are from a bit north of east. Do you see why this is so?

Now that we know how to measure some wave characteristics, we are ready to do the next investigation.

INVESTIGATING LONGSHORE CURRENTS

If you have ever tried floating on an air mattress near the edge of the beach, you know that you usually won't stay put for long. If there are waves striking the shore, you probably will be carried up or down the beach by a *longshore current.* A longshore current is a flow of water parallel to the beach and is caused by the waves striking the beach at an angle.

You can use almost any floating object to investigate longshore currents. Blocks of wood painted in bright colors or plastic milk jugs about half full of water work fine. You won't want to use anything that sticks out of the water so far that it is affected by the wind.

Drive two or three stakes into the beach in a row perpendicular to the shoreline, as shown in Figure 49. These stakes are used to line up the floats. Place another row of stakes about 50 feet (15 meters) up or down the beach. The direction of the second row, of course, will depend upon the direction of the long-shore current. If you don't know the direction, place one float in the water 20 to 30 feet (6 to 10 meters) offshore and watch which way it moves. An observer sighting down the second row of stakes will be able to see which floats cross the finish line first.

You will have to improvise to find a way to release the floats at the same time. One method is to run a heavy fishing line through the handles of the plastic milk jugs. One person wades out and holds the end of

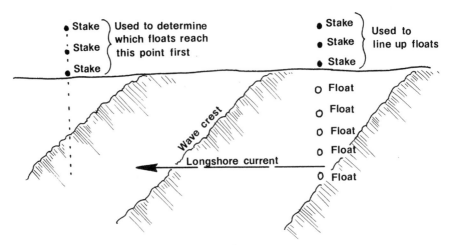

Figure 49. Floats placed in a row perpendicular to the beach can be used to investigate longshore currents.

the line. The floats should be at regular intervals along the line—say 10 feet (3 meters) apart. When the person in the water lets go of the line, another person on the shore pulls it in. The line slips through the plastic jugs and they are on their way! This method should be used only if the water is shallow and other conditions make it safe for the person to wade out with one end of the line.

Where is the longshore current stronger—near the shoreline or farther out? If you make measurements over a period of several days and keep good records, there are several questions you can tackle. Does the direction of the longshore current vary? Does the speed vary? Are the direction and speed of the long- shore current related to the direction of the wave movement? To the height of the waves?

94

INVESTIGATING WAVES IN THE SURF

A wave "feels" bottom when it moves across water shallower than one-half of its wavelength. For example, for a wave having a wavelength of 30 feet (10 meters), this happens when the water is about 15 feet (5 meters) deep. The bottom part of the wave is slowed by the friction between the water and the bottom. The top part of the wave moves forward at its regular speed. The result is a *breaker*, which forms when the wave spills over in front of its crest.

Figure 50 shows two types of breakers. The wave on the left in the diagram is breaking very quickly. The crest of this wave is thrown into the trough ahead of it and a *plunging breaker* is formed. If the wave breaks more slowly, the crest slides down the front of the wave and into the trough. This kind of breaker is called a *spilling breaker.*

There are many things that determine which kind of breaker will form—the slope of the seafloor, the shape of the waves approaching the shore, the offshore winds, and others. In general, spilling breakers are found where the slope of the seafloor is fairly gentle. Plunging breakers are found where the seafloor is steeper.

Plunging breaker   **Spilling breaker**
Figure 50.   Two types of breakers.

If you observe waves approaching a shoreline, you may see that part of the wave spills over. Other parts of the same wave may form a plunging breaker. This is a clue that some parts of the seafloor have a more gentle slope than others.

Where there are waves breaking, there often are surfers. Surfing began in Hawaii hundreds of years ago. Since then the sport has spread to most of the beaches of the world. If you don't have a fiberglass surfboard, you can easily use an air mattress or Styrofoam surfboard to investigate some of the science involved in this exciting sport.

At first riding the waves on a surfboard may seem to contradict what we learned earlier about waves. How can a surfer be propelled toward the shore if the water doesn't move forward as a wave passes? But we do know surfing is possible since we have seen surfers firsthand or watched them perform on television. And if you have played in the surf on an air mattress, you know how a wave can send you gliding toward the beach.

In many ways surfing is like riding a skateboard. A skateboard doesn't move if it's on a level spot. But when placed on a hill, the board and its passenger are in for a ride to the bottom.

Study Figure 51, which shows how a surfer gets started. Once he has "caught" the wave, he tries to keep himself positioned on the front side of the breaker. However, unlike the hill on which skateboarders ride, the wave moves forward with the surfer. For the surfer, it is not just a ride to the trough and the trip is over. By properly balancing himself and the

96

Figure 51. (a) The surfer paddles with his hands to gain speed. (b) Then he stands up when he feels a wave lift the surfboard. (c) Notice how he balances himself and keeps the board pointed downward as the wave carries him shoreward.

surfboard, the surfer can be carried all the way onto the beach.

You can check out these ideas by trying to get the longest ride possible on an air mattress or Styrofoam surfboard. You should get the best rides by properly balancing yourself and by positioning yourself on the front of a breaker.

Why do surfers ride on breakers and not on ordinary waves? The main reason is that breakers are higher than the waves from which they form. Also the front side of a breaker tends to be steeper than the sides of most waves along the shoreline.

Spilling breakers are better for surfing than plunging breakers because they last longer, or travel a greater distance. The famous surfboarding beaches at Waikiki in Hawaii have almost perfect spilling breakers. A very shallow and gently sloping seafloor goes out for more than a mile from the beach. Surfers can paddle out a long distance from the shore and be certain of a ride back on the almost endless succession of spilling breakers.

Plunging breakers in many ways are more exciting to watch than spilling breakers. Often the top of the wave curls over and traps air in the tunnel that forms in the front of the wave. The air is compressed and when it finally escapes, water may be hurled into the air higher than a house. Pictures of plunging breakers are often used in books and shown on television to illustrate the attractiveness of the seacoast.

DETERMINING THE HEIGHT OF BREAKERS

Before going in swimming, you may want to know how high the breakers are. In fact, it would be nice to know how deep the water is. Are there deep holes and are there sandbars offshore? Are there any currents that could be dangerous? By learning to read the waves you can get an idea of what the conditions are before you ever set foot in the water. Let's start by determining the height of breakers.

Figure 52 shows an easy way to measure the height of a breaker. Position yourself on a beach so your eye lines up with the top of the breaker and the horizon (where the sky meets the water). The height of the breaker is equal to the vertical distance between the eye and the average sea surface. The average sea surface is the level the water would be if it was not disturbed by waves, as on a calm day.

The average sea surface can be found in a number of ways. If the beach has a relatively constant slope, like the one in Figure 52, the procedure is as follows. Use a stick to mark the highest point the water runs up on the beach. It may be necessary to observe several successive waves and take an average. Use another stick to mark the lowest point on the beach where the sand is

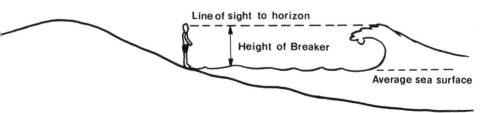

Figure 52. A simple way to estimate the height of a breaker.

99

exposed as the water runs back into the ocean. The average sea surface is approximately the point halfway between the upper and lower sticks. Of course, the average sea surface goes up and down as the tides come in and go out. You will have to find the average sea surface each time you want to measure the height of a breaker.

Following the breaking of each wave, a thin sheet of water called the *uprush* flows up the face of the beach. The uprush also is called the *swash.* Part of this water sinks into the sand and the rest runs back down the beach as *backrush.* As this backrush slides back toward the ocean, its speed increases. By the time it reaches a point a bit below the average level of the sea, a small wave about a foot high has formed. This small wave eventually curls over to form what is called a *backrush breaker.* The top of this backrush breaker also is approximately equal to the average sea surface.

Figure 53 shows how a friend can help you get a better estimate of the breaker heights. The friend holds

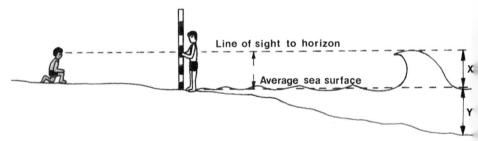

Figure 53. A stick like one used by surveyors improves the accuracy of the measurement of a breaker's height. The depth of the water (Y) is equal to 1.3 times the height of the breaker (X).

a stick upright and positions the bottom of the stick even with the average sea surface. As you sight the top of the breaker against the horizon, also note where this line of sight lines up on the stick. It will be helpful if the stick is painted like the ones used by surveyors— perhaps each foot of the stick painted alternately white and red or some other color. A stick painted this way can be used in later investigations to measure tides and to map the profile of a beach.

Have the person holding the stick place one hand on the stick so it lines up with the top of the breaker and the horizon. It will then be an easy job to measure to the bottom of the stick. This will give you a pretty good idea of how high the breakers really are.

Besides satisfying our natural curiosity about breakers, what good is this information about breaker height? Earlier we learned that the lower part of a wave starts to slow down or "feel" bottom when the wave enters water shallower than one-half of its wavelength. As the bottom slows and the top of the wave moves forward at its regular speed, a breaker is formed.

Scientists have found that a wave breaks when the depth of the water is 1.3 times the wave height. The wave height, of course, is the vertical distance from the crest to the trough of the wave (refer back to Figure 44). We can use this relationship between breaker height and water depth to calculate one if we know the other one. For example, if the breakers are 3 feet (90 centimeters) high, then the water depth at the point they are breaking is about 4 feet (120 centimeters). How do we know that? Remember, the depth of the water is equal to the breaker height multiplied by 1.3 (3 feet × 1.3 = approximately 4 feet).

We can use our new knowledge about breaker heights and water depths to predict the nature of the bottom offshore. And we won't have to get wet to do so. Let's take an example to see how this works. You notice the waves are breaking quite a distance offshore. Then as they move shoreward, they break a second time nearer the beach. What does this tell us about the ocean bottom?

The waves breaking offshore indicate that the water there is relatively shallow. If there is a long line of breakers, you may suspect this shallow water indicates an offshore sandbar. After the waves pass over the sandbar, they travel across deeper water and break a second time as they enter the shallower water near the beach. Figure 54 shows how this takes place.

If you watch a section of the beach over a period of time, the location of the breakers will probably change. This is not surprising, since the best word to describe any beach is the word *changing*. No beach

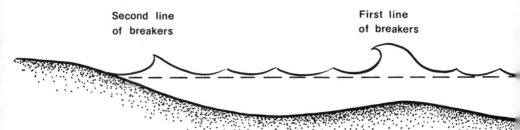

Figure 54. *The waves break first as they pass over the offshore sandbar on the right. A second line of breakers form as the waves enter the shallow water along the shoreline.*

stays the same for long, and this is especially true of sandy beaches. The waves striking a beach also are continuously changing. At one moment the sea may be calm and the water as smooth as a looking glass. A few hours later the surf is pounding the beach with all the force of a major storm.

If we look seaward and see only one line of breakers near the shoreline, we can't be sure what the bottom is like beyond the breakers. If the wind comes up and the waves increase in height, perhaps they will start breaking over an offshore bar. Or perhaps the tide is going out and as the average sea surface is lowered, the waves will break over the bar. It is necessary to observe a section of the beach for several hours or even days to get a good picture of the ocean bottom along the shore. And even then you may be wrong because things are always changing—sand on the bottom is shifting, tides vary in height, storms at sea create giant waves, and the direction of the wind shifts. It is because of all these factors that studying waves is such a fascinating subject.

BEWARE! UNDERTOW!

Have you ever seen a sign like the one in Figure 55 posted along a beach? Or perhaps you have been warned about going into the ocean when the surf is up. Many people fear they will be pulled under by "undertow" and carried out to sea.

We can apply what we have learned about waves and the ocean bottom along the shoreline to understand what some people call *undertow*. If you watch the water run back down the beach after a wave has

Figure 55. Have you ever seen a sign like this?

come in, it is not difficult to imagine how the idea of undertow originated. The water carried up on the beach by incoming waves must go someplace. Some sinks in the sand and the rest runs back down to the ocean as backrush. The bigger the waves, the more water that is carried up on to the beach, and the greater amount of backrush. It seems reasonable that this sheet of water moving back toward the ocean might carry a person with it. In fact, you can feel its force against your legs when you stand in the edge of the surf. However, scientists do not use the term *undertow* because they don't believe it exists. Instead, they have another way of explaining what happens when a swimmer is swept out to sea.

If the bottom of the ocean uniformly slopes away from the beach, the amount of water running back to the ocean at any one spot usually is not enough to cause a serious problem for swimmers. However, if there are offshore bars with breaks in them, the currents produced could easily be strong enough to be dangerous. Let's take a typical summer day at the beach to see how this works.

The early riser often sees the ocean as calm as a small pond on a quiet day. The surface of the ocean is broken only by the splashes of some feeding fish. As the sun rises higher in the sky, breezes spring up and ripple the water as they move shoreward. The wind increases as the day wears on and the waves get higher and higher. By afternoon the larger waves are breaking as they cross the sandbar some distance offshore. Now conditions are right for a dangerous situation to develop!

The water being piled up between the offshore bar and the beach must somehow return to the sea. Figure 56 shows what happens when there are breaks or gaps in the offshore bar, which often is the case. Since the water in the area of the gaps is deeper, waves approaching the shore do not break there. Water returning to the sea does not encounter as much resistance where there are no breakers, and currents like those shown in Figure 56 are the result. The currents are called *rip currents*.

Scientists studying rip currents think of these movements of water as intense bottlenecks of energy. They are strongest near the breaker zone and broaden and weaken as they reach out to sea (see Figure 56). They seldom extend farther than 100 yards (100 meters) offshore and usually are not more than 10 yards wide.

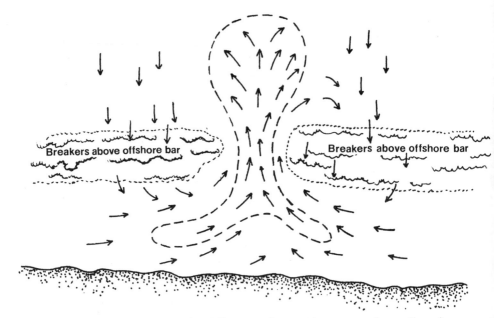

Breakers above offshore bar

Breakers above offshore bar

Figure 56. The dashed line encloses the area where the rip current is strongest and generally moving seaward.

However, these currents extend from the top of the water to the ocean bottom. Do you see how they differ from what is suggested by the word *undertow*, which would be a current on the ocean floor?

Rip currents are clearly visible from a height, such as from the top of a dune or cliff or from a low-flying airplane. Sometimes they can be seen from the beach also. One thing to look for is change in water color. Water in a rip current may be a brownish color because of the heavy load of sand it is carrying. Or it may be greener than the surrounding water because of the greater depth of the water in areas favoring the formation of a rip current. Because the current is flowing against the overall movement of the water along the shoreline, the water surface is often stirred up, with whitecaps extending beyond the breaker zone. There also may be a gap in the breakers where a rip current is forcing its way seaward. Sometimes a line of foam also signals a dangerous rip current, and this is especially true along rocky coasts.

Perhaps the easiest way to detect a rip current is to observe a floating object in the water. If the object bobs up and down with the waves and moves slowly shoreward, there is no rip current at that particular location. However, if the object moves rapidly seaward, a rip current probably exists. You may wish to toss a piece of wood painted a bright color or a plastic milk jug into the surf at various locations to see if you can detect any rip currents.

Rip currents present a real threat to the safety of those who swim in the surf. The best precaution to take is to know the conditions that produce rip currents and avoid the surf when these conditions are present. As we have seen, rip currents are produced when the waves are breaking. Some experts say, as a rule of thumb, that conditions may be considered dangerous to swimmers when one out of every three waves breaks over an offshore bar. This condition often occurs in the afternoon when the wind is blowing toward the land. However, storms at sea, often hundreds of miles away, can cause high waves along the seacoast any time of day or night.

The tides also play a role in the creation of rip currents. An incoming or *flooding tide* may cover the bar to such a depth that waves pass over it without breaking. They run up on the beach and the return flow of water runs back more or less evenly along the beach. An outgoing or *ebb tide* has the opposite effect. The water over the bar is lower and the waves are more likely to break. Also the bottom near the shoreline during ebb tide is more likely to concentrate the returning water and form rip currents.

Generally speaking, it is safest to swim in the morning and when the tide is coming in. The wind is usually less strong, and the waves are not as high. An afternoon when there is an outgoing tide is likely to be the most dangerous. Winds are often the greatest and the waves the highest during that part of the day.

What should swimmers do if caught in a rip current? *Do not* try to swim shoreward against the current! The current may be moving seaward at speeds of 2 or 3 miles (3 to 5 kilometers) per hour. Instead of swimming toward the shore, it is recommended that those caught in a rip current swim parallel to the shore. The current is quite narrow at the point where it is strongest (See Figure 56). Often the water only a few yards or meters to either side of the rip current is safe and the bottom shallow. If unable to break away from the current, swimmers should stay afloat and ride with it until its speed decreases. Then they should be able to reach safety by swimming diagonally toward the shore.

Experts recommend that nonswimmers should not get into water deeper than their knees. If bathers wearing life jackets are caught in a rip current, they should call for help and try to stay calm. The life jacket will support them until someone can throw a rope and tow them in. As has been recommended several times already in this book, practice the "buddy system," and preferably with someone who is a good swimmer. Never swim alone—if you are caught in a rip current, there will be no one to help you. And of course the best advice is to avoid swimming in the surf when conditions favor the formation of rip currents.

INVESTIGATING TIDES

When is the fishing best along the coast? What is the best time to go shelling? When are rip currents most likely to form? The tides must be considered in answering these questions and many others. The tides affect almost everything that happens along our seashores and often many miles inland along the shores of rivers and bays.

How often do we have a high tide and a low tide? What is the difference between the average sea surface, or water level, at high tide and at low tide? These and other questions about tides are fairly easy to investigate. However, an open beach is not necessarily the best place to start. An open beach would be fine if there were no wind and waves. But this is usually not the case. The waves make it difficult to determine very accurately when the average sea surface is highest and when it is lowest.

Often there is a protected area of water near the beach—a bay, marsh, or other body of water that is connected directly to the open ocean. This would be a good place to start your investigations of tides. After you have taken measurements in a protected area, you can always repeat the measurements in other locations.

Your results probably will vary a bit from those obtained on the open beach. But this won't matter since the main purpose of the investigations is to determine the patterns of the tides for your part of the country.

Begin by attaching a measuring stick to a piling or other structure in the body of water you plan to use. Or you may wish to drive into the bottom a long stick that can be used as a tidal gauge. It will work best if you fasten some type of measuring instrument (yardstick, meterstick, tape measure, etc.) to the stick. Or you can use a pencil to mark the stick off in inches or centimeters before you place it in the water (see Figure 57).

Figure 57. The height of low and high tide can be determined by using a tape measure fastened to a dock or to a stick placed in the water.

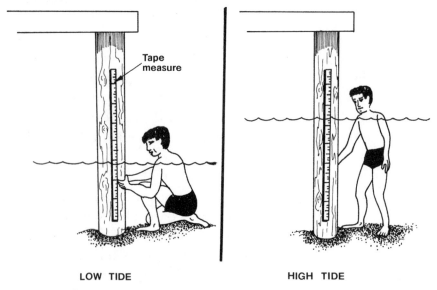

LOW TIDE   HIGH TIDE

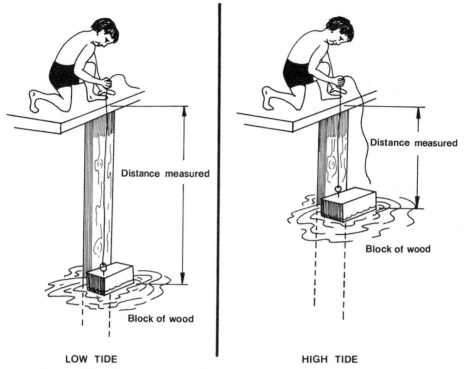

LOW TIDE   HIGH TIDE

Figure 58. Another way of determining the height of low and high tides is to lower a block of wood until it floats in the water.

If it is not possible to get into the water to install your tidal gauge and to take readings, there are other ways the data can be obtained. If the surface of the water is smooth, you can use a rope or heavy cord to lower a block of wood from a dock (see Figure 58). Lower the wooden block slowly until it reaches the water and floats. Use a tape measure or yardstick to measure the length of the rope required to lower the block to the water's surface. In analyzing your data, remember that the tide will be highest when the distance from the water's surface to the top of the dock is least. Do you see why this is so?

What if you want to measure the height of the water level when there are waves? The wooden block and rope method shown in Figure 58 can be changed a bit to allow you to do this. You will need a cardboard, plastic, or metal tube. The tube should be from 3 to 6 inches (8 to 15 centimeters) across and about 6 feet (2 meters) long. The diameter, or distance across the tube, is not too important. However, the tube must be longer than the distance between low and high tide. Cardboard tubes that rugs come rolled around, plastic drainpipes used by plumbers, or metal pipes used on furnaces all will work. Or you can use some boards to build a long wooden box that is open on one end.

Close off one end of the tube with a wooden plug or by some other means. Drill a few holes about one-half inch (one centimeter) in diameter near the closed-off end. Attach the tube to a post under a dock as shown in Figure 59. The tube must be in an upright position and the end with the small holes must be below the water level at low tide.

The water is free to flow into and out of the tube, but not at a very fast rate. As a result, the water level inside the tube changes very little, even though the water level outside changes a great deal as each wave passes. The height of the water level inside the tube can be measured by lowering a floating object inside the tube as shown in Figure 59.

Regardless of which method you use to measure the

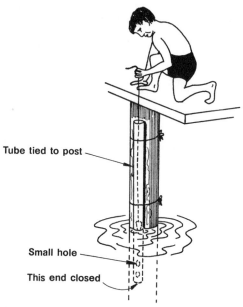

Tube tied to post

Small hole

This end closed

*Figure 59. Here is a method of determining the height of the
water level when there are waves on the water.*

height of the water level, you will need to make
observations over a period of several hours in order to
study tidal patterns. Record the time of day and the
height of the water on your tidal gauge each time you
make an observation. You may wish to use a table like
Table 1 in which to record your data.

Table 1

TIDES IN NEW YORK HARBOR

(Measured with a Tape Measure Fastened to a Stick)

Date	Time	Height (Feet and Inches)
June 22	8:00 A.M.	8'9"
	9:00	9'0"
	10:00	8'6"
	11:00	7'0"
	12:00 (noon)	6'2"
	1:00 P.M.	5'7"
	2:00	5'3"
	3:00	5'1"
	4:00	5'2"
	5:00	5'8"
	6:00	7'0"
	7:00	8'2"
	8:00	9'1"
	9:00	9'8"
	10:00	9'11"
	11:00	9'7"
June 23	12:00 (midnight)	8'9"
	1:00 A.M.	7'8"
	2:00	6'9"
	3:00	6'0"
	4:00	5'6"
	5:00	5'7"
	6:00	6'4"
	7:00	6'8"
	8:00	7'6"
	9:00	8'4"
	10:00	8'9"

Look at the data in Table 1. About when did any high tides occur? When did low tides occur? Can you estimate, to the nearest hour, the length of time between a high tide and the next low tide? Between a high tide and the next high tide? The difference in the level of the water at low tide and at high tide?

Now that you have some idea of tidal patterns, can you find answers to these questions for your own particular location? Be sure to keep neat and accurate records of all your observations. And, if possible, make your observations more often than each hour. The more readings you take, the more accurately you will be able to predict when the high and low tides actually occurred. Do you see why this is so?

What if you can't take your readings at regular time intervals? For example, sometimes your readings are fifteen minutes apart, other times they are an hour or more apart. This is not a major problem: you can draw a graph of your data. Besides, a graph is often the best way to find out what the data shows.

Figure 60 is a graph of the data recorded in Table 1 of the tides in New York Harbor. Notice how height of the water level is marked off on the left side of the graph. Time is shown across the bottom of the graph. Each of the dots on the graph corresponds to one of the readings in Table 1. By connecting the dots with a line, it is easier to figure out when high and low tides occurred. The line also helps in estimating the difference in the water levels at high and low tides.

Perhaps the results you obtained differ a great deal from those shown in Table 1 and in Figure 60. Tides

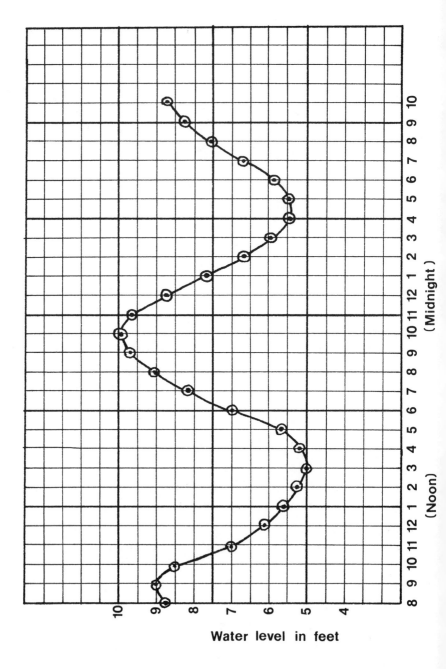

Figure 60. The tides in New York Harbor.

116

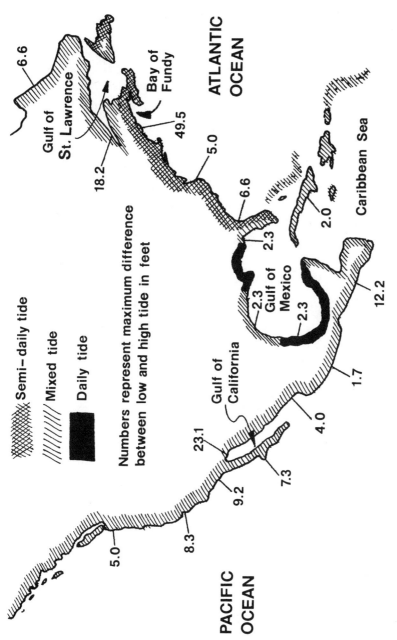

Figure 61. These are the kinds of tides along the coast of North America.

do not occur everywhere on a twice-a-day cycle. Nor do tides in many locations show such a regular pattern. The map in Figure 61 shows the kind of tides that occur in much of the Northern Hemisphere.

A word of explanation probably is needed about the different kinds of tides. *Semidaily tides* are like those in New York Harbor. High tides there are about a half-day apart and most days there are two high tides. Also the height of the water level at each high tide is about the same.

Some places, like much of the coast along the Gulf of Mexico, have only one high tide each day. These are called *daily tides*. A graph of the tides at Pensacola, Florida, is shown in Figure 62. Notice the daily pattern. Also notice that there isn't much difference there between high and low tides.

Locations along the Pacific Coast and in Hawaii have *mixed tides*. This means there are two high tides each day, but the height of the water at high tide varies. Every other high tide is much greater than the one in between. Study the graphs of tides at San Diego, California and Honolulu, Hawaii. Do you see why they are considered to be mixed tides?

Many newspapers report the time of each low and high tide at certain locations in their part of the country. Tide tables giving this information also are available at many bait shops and other places along the seacoast. How do the results you obtained compare with those reported in these tide tables?

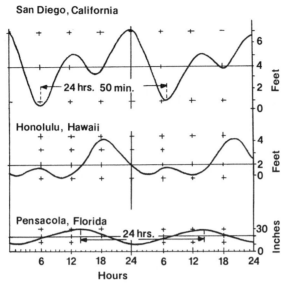

Figure 62. This is a graph of the tides in three locations in the United States.

CAUSES OF TIDES AND MORE INVESTIGATIONS

You may have noticed that the tides are much higher at some times than they are at others. Also the length of time between tides may vary at your location. These and many other things can be investigated by taking regular readings of the water level at a location over a period of days or weeks. Or you can use the tide tables for your location to find out more about some of these things.

Tides are caused mainly by the gravitational attraction of the sun and the moon on the earth. Understanding how this works should suggest several more questions about tides to investigate.

119

Look first at the diagram on the left in Figure 63. This is the situation when there is a new moon, or the sun and moon are on the same side of the earth. The combined gravitational attraction of the sun and moon on the waters of the oceans produces a very high tide called a *spring tide.*

Since it takes twenty-four hours for the earth to make one rotation, many people unfamiliar with the seacoast expect a high tide only once a day. We have seen that this is true in some places, such as along much of the coastline of the Gulf of Mexico (see

Figure 63.   Spring tides occur when the earth, moon, and sun are in a straight line.

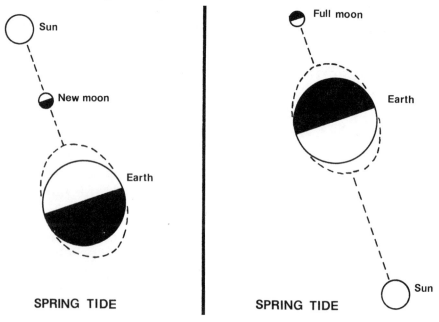

Figure 61). But most places have two high tides each day, or high tide about every twelve hours.

Figure 63 should help you understand why this is so. Because of the gravitational force of the moon and sun, the water is pulled away from the earth. A bulge forms on the side of the earth facing the sun and moon. However, a bulge also forms on the other side of the earth, as shown in Figure 63. In this case the earth is believed to be pulled away from the water.

Now look at the right side of Figure 63. This is the situation at full moon. (This is fourteen days later than the new-moon situation shown on the left of Figure 63.) We also have spring tides at the time of full moon, or when earth, sun, and moon are in a straight line.

Figure 64 shows the situation when the moon is at

Figure 64. *Neap tides occur when the sun, earth, and moon are at right angles to each other.*

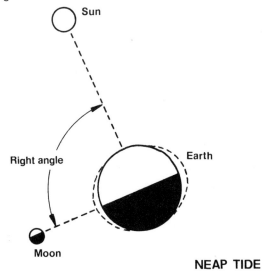

first quarter or third quarter. Notice how the sun, earth, and moon are at right angles to each other. Tides during this period are called *neap tides*. Are neap tides generally greater or less than spring tides?

You can see that the moon plays a very important role in causing tides. There are some other things about tides you can use the position of the moon to investigate. The next time there is a full moon, observe the time the moon rises for several nights in a row. You should find that it rises about fifty minutes later each night. If we used the moon instead of the sun as a basis of time, each day would be about twenty-four hours and fifty minutes long.

Look at the data you have collected on tides in your part of the country. What is the average length of time between one high tide and the next one? How does this check out with the tide curves in Figures 60 and 62? Does the period between high tides in places having semidaily tides match up more closely with the apparent motion of the sun or the moon? What is the period between high tides in places having daily tides? In places having mixed tides?

Here are a few more things you can investigate. Each year we have what is called a harvest moon in late September or early October. This is a full moon that rises at about the same time each night for several nights in a row. What is the length of time between high tides during the harvest moon?

Since the moon revolves around the earth in an egg-shaped orbit, its distance from the earth varies— from about 220,000 miles (352,000 kilometers) to about 250,000 miles (400,000 kilometers). What effect does the varying distance between the earth and the moon have on tides? (Find the distance from the earth to the moon on a particular day in an astronomical reference book and check this out.)

As you see, explaining the many ways that tides vary can become rather complicated. And scientists cannot explain all the things they have observed about tides. Nevertheless, tides play a very important role in what happens along a beach. In trying to explain what is happening there, always ask yourself if tides are involved in whatever it is you are observing.

MAPPING THE BEACH'S PROFILE

The waves and currents of the ocean are in constant attack against the beaches of the world. If the beach consists mainly of boulders and other large rocks, changes in the shape of the beach occur slowly. This is not so with sandy beaches. These beaches are in a constant state of change, even from day to day. To understand some of the things that are happening on a sandy beach, we must map an accurate picture of the beach's profile.

Select a place on the beach where it will be convenient to do this investigation and several that follow. It will be helpful if there is some fixed object you can use as a reference point. A post placed in the edge of a dune will allow you to return to the same spot for more measurements. The top of the post or a mark on it can be used as a vertical reference point. You may want to find out how the height of the beach is changing over a period of time.

To map the profile of the beach, you can use a

method much like that used to survey land. The equipment you will need is not expensive, though. Two sticks, one about 6 feet (2 meters) long and the other about 12 feet (4 meters) long will do. You also will need the help of a friend to hold one of the sticks. A third person to record the data will speed things up.

Use your heel or a stick to draw a straight line in the sand from your reference point to the edge of the beach. This is the line along which you will be taking measurements. Next shove one end of the shorter stick into the sand. It should be straight up and down and should be tall enough so it is comfortable for you to sight across the top of it (as shown in Figure 65). Mark the sighting stick so you will know how far it is in the sand. Also measure the distance from the surface of the sand to the top of the sighting stick. The sighting stick must be pushed into the sand to the same depth each time you use it. Otherwise your readings taken over a period of time cannot be compared. Do you see why this is so?

If you have a reference point like the post in Figure 65, also record the distance from the top of the reference point to the top of the sighting stick.

Pace off 5 yards (about 5 meters) from the sighting stick, as shown in Figure 65. A long step or pace is about a yard. Have a friend hold the longer stick so its bottom just touches the sand. As in the earlier investigation of breaker height, the stick will be easier to use if every other foot is painted a different color. Red and

Figure 65. *This is a method of determining the profile of a beach (each square represents one foot).*

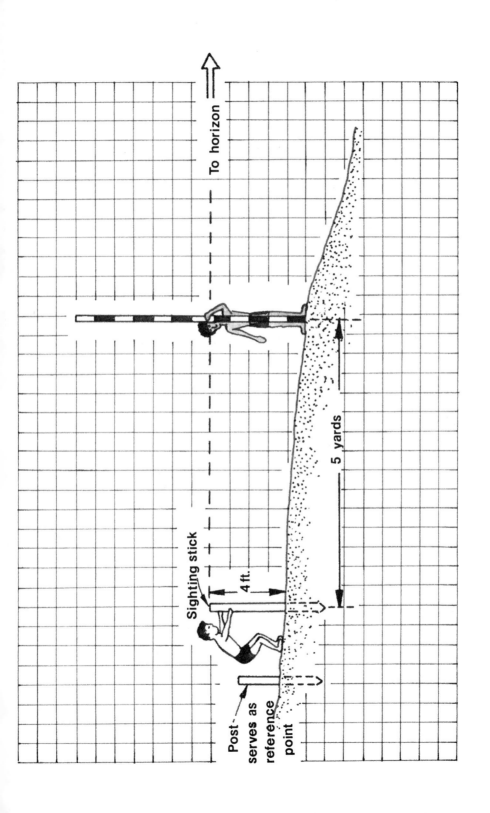

white are good colors to use, but you can use any contrasting colors.

Sight across the top of the sighting stick toward the horizon as shown in Figure 65. The broken line in Figure 65 represents a line that is level and from which we can make vertical measurements. Have the person holding the longer stick slide one hand up or down the stick until it lines up with the line extending to the horizon. If the person can't reach this high, a short stick can be held up alongside the longer one. Surveyors have a device that can be slid up and down the longer stick. Perhaps you can invent such a device to place on your longer stick.

Record the distance from the person's hand on the stick to the bottom of the stick. You may want to record your data using a table like Table 2.

After you have made a measurement at Position A, have the person holding the longer stick move another 5 yards down the line extending toward the water. Measure the distance of this position from the sight line to the horizon. Keep repeating this process until the person holding the long stick reaches the edge of the water. If you want to map the profile of the ocean bottom near the shore, continue taking measurements. However, the person holding the longer stick should not go into the water when it is unsafe to do so.

Often the easiest way to understanding something is by drawing a picture or graph. Figure 66 is a graph of the data recorded in Table 2. In Figure 66 each square represents one yard. You may want to draw your graphs on a large piece of paper or on several pieces of

Table 2

MEASUREMENTS OF A BEACH PROFILE

Position	Height (Feet and Inches)
Top of sighting stick above the sand	4'
Top of sighting stick above the top of the post used as a reference point	1'4"
Position A (5 yards from sighting stick)	5'
Position B (10 yards)	8'6"
Position C (15 yards)	9'4"
Position D (20 yards)	10'2"
Position E (25 yards)	12'

graph paper taped together. By letting each square represent one foot, you would be able to get a better picture of the beach you are investigating.

If you are mapping a wide beach or one with a steep slope, it may be necessary to move your sighting stick one or more additional times. In a situation like the one shown in Figure 66, you could move it to Position E (water's edge). Then you could go ahead and map

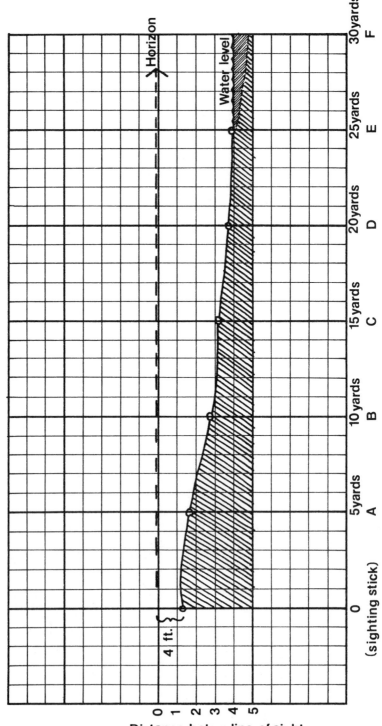

the shallow water extending out from the edge of the beach. However, you would have to add 12 feet to your readings taken in the water (the difference in elevation of the top of the sighting stick at the beginning and at Position E). If you have difficulty in figuring out how much to add when you move the sighting stick, draw a picture of your situation. The amount added is the difference between the elevation of the two positions at which you place the sighting stick.

Determining the profile of one spot on the beach doesn't tell you too much. But if you repeat your measurements in several places on the beach, there are several questions you may be able to answer. If the beach curves, where is it steepest? In what places is the beach the widest? Does the direction the beach faces make any difference? What is the relationship between the slope of the beach and the kind of ocean bottom at a particular place?

Or better yet, make your measurements of a beach over a period of weeks or months. How does the profile of the beach change over a period of time? What is the effect of storms and big waves? How is the profile of the beach different in the summer and in the winter?

You can answer many of the these questions by just observing the beach. But it is more fun to take measurements and keep good records. This will allow you to detect many changes you might otherwise miss.

Figure 66. Beach profile obtained by drawing a graph of the data in Table 2 (each square equals one yard).

BEACH STUDY GIVES CLUES TO THE PAST

Many of the things that can be observed on a beach are of special interest to geologists and other scientists who study the history of the earth. Geologists get many of their clues to what the earth was like millions of years ago by studying sedimentary rocks. These rocks are made up of sediments much like the material you find along a sandy beach. (Sediments are the solid materials carried by moving water or the wind, and which settle out to form layers.) By studying the sediments of the beach you can learn about what is happening there and at the same time learn about how geologists work.

Begin by collecting a sample of water from a wave as it strikes the beach. Also collect a sample of water from the backrush, or the water that runs back down the beach after a wave has come in. Be sure to label your samples so you will know when and where you collected them.

The next step is to remove the water from the samples. You can let the water evaporate, but you probably won't want to wait that long. Perhaps a better way is to use a cloth or piece of nylon stocking to strain the samples.

Place the sediments obtained from each sample on a piece of paper toweling to dry. Once they are dry, examine them carefully. Are there differences in the shape, size, and color of the particles in the various sediments? If you have a microscope or hand lens, by all means use it in your observations.

Geologists have found the size of the particles carried by moving water is an indication of how fast the water is moving. A rapidly flowing stream can carry particles much larger than those carried by a stream with little current. Does what you found out about the sediments carried by incoming waves and by the backrush support this idea? Generally the water in the incoming waves is moving more rapidly than the water in the backrush.

Next collect a sample of the sand from the beach and place it in a glass or clear plastic container. Sand composed of various-sized particles will work best in this investigation. Fill the container with water and stir. Place the container where it will not be disturbed and allow the solid materials to settle to the bottom. Which particles settle to the bottom first? Last?

If you aren't sure, perhaps you can answer the question by examining the top and bottom particles with a hand lens or microscope. Or you can add some material made up of larger particles and stir up the contents of the container again.

The fact that the larger particles settle down first is a very important piece of information. If a rapidly moving stream slows down, the larger, heavier particles in the water will settle down first. Let's apply this to beaches.

Collect samples of sand from various parts of a beach. If you have already mapped the profile of the beach in a certain area, you may wish to make your collection there. If possible, use a hand lens or microscope to examine your samples. Are the particles in the various samples all the same size? If not, where are the largest ones found? How can your findings be explained? Does the velocity of the water from which the sediments were deposited have anything to do with what you found out? What other factors, such as the wind, may have been involved?

What is the beach like beneath its surface? To find out, dig a series of holes 5 to 10 yards apart starting at the edge of the water. The holes should be in a straight line perpendicular to the shoreline. Square holes a yard or so across work best. Since a later investigation (p. 140) of the water table also involves digging holes, you may want to do that one at the same time.

Avoid digging holes in the dunes that are found along the many beaches. In many states it is against the law to do so. A dune is very fragile, or easily destroyed. Preserving the dunes is very important since during a storm they help protect the area behind the dunes.

Use a flat shovel or large knife to make the sides of the holes straight up and down and smooth. Can you see any layers? If so, are they level or do they slope? Which way do they slope? Are they all the same thickness? Are they all the same color? Do the layers appear to be made of sediments of varying sizes? Of sediments of differing materials?

The layers provide clues to what the conditions were like when the sediments were deposited. For example, during a storm there are high waves and large particles are washed up on the beach. On a less noticeable scale, the coarse sand deposited by the surf as the tide goes out is covered by the finer sand deposited by the backrush. Can you suggest what may have caused the layers you observed? This is very similar to what geologists do in trying to explain the layers they find in many rocks. These rock layers often can be observed where a highway has been cut through a hill or mountain.

You may wish to make a sketch or take a picture of any layers you uncover. This way you can make comparisons over a period of time. How is the beach different after a storm? Before and after a high tide? During the summer and during the winter?

In addition to sketches and photographs, there is another way of making a record of the layers. Coat a piece of stiff cardboard or plywood with some clear glue or varnish. You may need to give it a second coat if the first one is absorbed. When the coating feels "tacky," press the coated side of the cardboard against the side of one of your holes in the beach. Hold it there firmly for a few minutes and then very carefully pull it away. The sand trapped in the glue or varnish makes a good permanent record. In addition, you can scrape off particles for later study under a microscope.

Be sure to fill in the holes you dig. True, they will probably be filled in by the incoming tide, but meanwhile, someone might fall in a hole and injure him- or herself. Besides, a good investigator always leaves an area as undisturbed as possible.

STUDYING THE FACE OF THE BEACH

The face or surface of the beach as well as its profile is constantly changing. If you don't believe this, watch a small section of the beach near the water's edge for a few minutes. Each wave carries new particles up onto the beach. As the water runs back to the ocean, some of the beach is carried with it.

This almost continuous movement of water and sand produces some interesting results. Many of these are easily observed on a sandy beach. A good time to look is early in the morning when the tide is going out. The high tide will have erased any marks made by people the previous day.

Figure 67 should help you find *ripple marks.* Although they vary in size and shape, many are diamond shaped and a couple of inches across. Look for ripple marks in the shallow water along the edge of the surf. Also look on the face of gently sloping beaches when the tide is out.

Ripple marks are found wherever there is sand under moving water. They have been photographed on the ocean floor in water thousands of feet deep. Ripple marks are also found preserved in layers of sedimentary rock, sometimes alongside dinosaur tracks. You can see why geologists are interested in ripple marks.

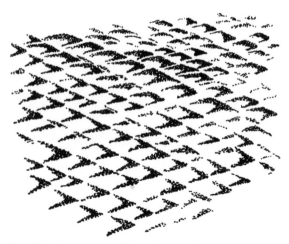

Figure 67. Ripple marks like these often can be observed in shallow water and/or the face of the beach during low tide.

If they know the conditions that cause ripple marks to form now, they can figure out what the floor of the sea was like millions of years ago when the dinosaurs lived on the earth.

Swash marks (see Figure 68) are lines on the beach that mark the uppermost movement of the swash, or uprush. This is the thin sheet of water that runs up on the beach as a wave comes in. This thin sheet of water bulldozes a line of sand particles ahead of it. When the

Figure 68. Swash marks are lines on the beach that mark the uppermost movement of the water from a wave.

135

water retreats back down the beach, these sand particles are left behind as a record of where the water had
been. Examine some of the particles in a swash mark.
Are they larger or smaller than the sand particles found
nearby?

Backrush marks (see Figure 69) are made as the
water runs back down the beach to the ocean. These
are diamond-shaped patterns, with each diamond
about 6 inches (15 centimeters) long. The long part of
the diamond also points seaward and the short point is

*Figure 69. Backrush marks like these sometimes form as the
water from a wave runs back down the beach to the ocean.*

parallel to the face of the beach. Backrush marks are
most likely to be found in fairly coarse sand on a beach
of medium steepness. Why these backrush marks take
the shape that they do is still a mystery.

Rills (see Figure 70) sometimes form on a beach as the tide ebbs, or goes out. Water trapped in the upper part of the beach slowly seeps out and runs down the face of the beach. As it does, it forms thousands of miniature streams. These streams carve out channels in the sand much in the same way a large stream wears away the land.

1 2 3 4 5 6 7 8 9 10 11 12
Scale in inches

Figure 70. Rills look much like the stem and branches of a plant (turn drawing upside down if you don't see a resemblance).

Look closely at any rills you can find on the beach. Notice how they spread out near the lower part of their journey down the face of the beach. This is much like the way many rivers branch as they reach their deltas. (*Deltas* are low-lying flat areas made up of materials deposited by a river as it flows into the sea.) Some people have found rills in ancient rocks and thought they were fossil plants. Note how they do look like the outline of a plant with its stem pointing shoreward.

Sand domes and *pinholes* (see Figure 71) remind many people of oatmeal being cooked. And in many ways they are alike. In oatmeal, bubbles form near the bottom of the pan where it is hottest and then rise to the top. When the bubbles reach the surface, they break and leave the oatmeal covered with marks.

As the tide comes in, the swash comes farther and farther up on the beach. Much of this water sinks into the dry sand of the upper part of the beach. The air trapped in the sand rises as a series of small bubbles. These bubbles form small pinholes in the sand. Watch

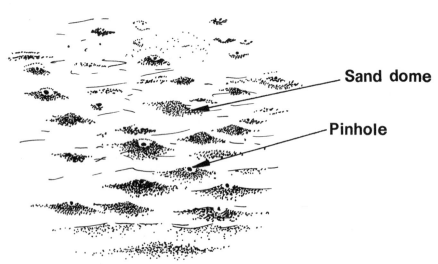

Figure 71. Sand domes and pinholes are formed by the pressure of water on pockets of air trapped in the sand.

carefully and you will see the bubbles escape from these holes.

When more water sinks into the sand, the pinholes are sealed. The air trapped in the sand cannot escape and forms larger and larger bubbles. As the pressure of the water on these air bubbles increases, the bubbles push the sand above them into small domes. These domes are usually about ½ inch (1 centimeter) high and 3 inches (8 centimeters) across.

Ripple marks, swash marks, pinholes, and sand domes are all rather faintly written messages on the face of the beach. Because they are small many people walk on a beach without even noticing them. This is not the case with *cusps*. Cusps are so large that it is hard to miss seeing them.

Figure 72 shows cusps along a beach in California.

Figure 72.   *Cusps give the edge of a beach a scalloped look.*

They vary in shape, but always give the edge of the beach a scalloped look. They vary in size from a few inches across to more than a thousand feet from point to point. Scientists do not agree on what causes cusps to form the way they do. The height of waves and the direction from which they approach the shore seems to have something to do with it.

The formation of backrush marks and cusps isn't the only mystery of the beach face that remains unsolved. However, it illustrates a very important characteristic of science: there is no end to the questions about nature.

SAND CASTLES AND WATER TABLES

Few people can resist the temptation to dig a hole in a sandy beach. Some spend hours building huge sand castles, only to have them destroyed in minutes by the incoming tide. There are many scientific ideas that can be investigated while digging holes and building sand castles. One of these deals with the water table.

Dig a hole in the upper part of the beach at high tide. Once you have dug though the layer of dry sand, you will come to damp sand. Keep digging. The deeper you dig, the wetter the sand becomes. If you dig deep enough, water will flow into the hole. The level of water in a hole is called the *water table.*

Dig another hole lower on the beach. How does the water table in this hole compare with the water table in the first hole you dug? Continue digging a series of holes down the face of the beach. The last hole should be near the edge of the water. How does the water level in each of these holes compare to that in the first hole you dug? Are your results similar to those shown in Figure 73? Can you draw a picture like Figure 73 to show the water table on the beach where you are doing your investigation?

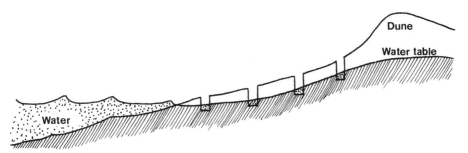

Figure 73. The water table can be found by digging holes and observing the level of the water standing in them.

If you started your investigation at high tide, notice what happens to the water table as the tide goes out. The level of water in the holes will change more slowly than the level of the water in the ocean. This is because it takes a while for the water to seep through the sand and back into the ocean. Is the opposite true when the tide is coming in? How does the amount the water table changes compare with the difference between low and high tide at your location?

Of what importance is the water table? For one thing, it tells us how deep a well must be dug in order to get water. Along the beach the water table is fairly close to the surface. Some vacation homes depend on pipes driven a few feet into the sand for their supply of water. And what surprises many people is that wells only a few hundred feet from the beach produce fresh water. This fresh water is pushed up by a more dense layer of salt water under it. Make your well too deep and you will get salt water instead of fresh water.

Later you will learn how to build an instrument to measure the amount of salt in the water. You may wish to use this instrument to test the water in the series of holes you have dug on the beach. Or you can wet your finger with water from the hole and taste it to see how salty it is.

Be sure to fill in the holes once you have finished your observations.

SINKING BEACH CHAIRS

Anyone who has visited a sandy beach probably has not passed up the chance to get his or her feet wet. If you stand in the water less than knee deep, you may have experienced a strange sensation. You feel yourself slowly sink! Are you caught in a pool of quicksand? Will you slowly sink out of sight?

You also may have had the same sinking experience in a beach chair along the water's edge. The sand seems firm and you lie back in the chair for a short nap. Then the tide starts coming in and the sand under the chair gets wetter and wetter. When does the chair start to sink? Try it.

The sand along the water's edge is stirred up by the action of the waves. Rather than solid sand, you are on a layer of sand and water. It is not surprising that you sink. But how far do you sink? Usually only a few inches, because only that much of the sand is being stirred up by the water.

When do you sink the most? When a wave is coming in or when the backrush runs back down the beach? When a tide is coming in or going out? When the waves are high or when there is little surf? When the waves are striking the beach at an angle? These are a few questions you can investigate while sitting in a sinking beach chair.

The ability of a solid object to pass through sand with a high water content is put to good use by builders. How can a post be sunk into a sandy beach? One way is to pound it in. But there is an easier way.

People who build piers and other structures in the water or along a sandy beach often use pumps. The post is placed upright, as shown in Figure 74. A stream of water is directed toward the sand under the post. The sand is stirred up, as in the case of the beach chair

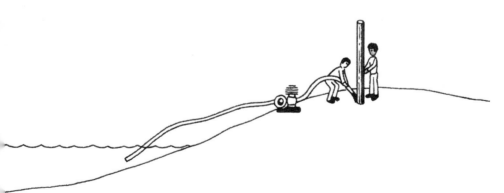

Figure 74.   A post can be sunk into a sandy beach by directing a stream of water at its base.

in the surf, and the post slowly sinks. Turn off the water and the post remains in place.

You can try this with a garden hose if you have one in a place where there is a lot of sand. Place the nozzle of the hose next to a stick that is in a vertical position. Push down on the stick as the water from the hose fills the surrounding area with water. Do not turn off the water while the hose is in the sand. If you do so, the water in the sand will quickly drain away and the end of the hose as well as the stick will be trapped in the sand.

WHY DO THE WINDS ALWAYS BLOW?

If you have ever spent much time at the beach or along the shore of a large lake, you probably have noticed that there is a breeze most of the time. What keeps the air in almost constant motion? And why does the wind generally blow toward the land in the daytime and toward the water at night? These questions can be investigated easily near any large body of water. The answers will help you explain many of the weather phenomena we have here on the earth.

The main things you will need for this investigation are several thermometers to take air, water, and soil temperatures. You can get by with one thermometer, but it will take more time to do the investigation. Also needed is a means of determining wind speed and direction. In addition, it will be helpful to have a watch or clock so you can make your observations at regular intervals.

While taking temperatures it is important that the sun not strike the thermometer directly. The temperatures reported in the newpapers and on radio and TV are temperatures taken in the shade. While taking water and air temperatures, you can hold the thermometer so it is in your shadow. In the case of soil temperatures, you may want to prop up boards or other objects so their shadows shade the thermometers, but not the soil.

There are several ways to go about finding the direction and speed of the wind. Throw up a handful of dry sand and notice which way the wind carries it. If the sand is blown toward the east, we say the wind is out of the west. We always describe wind direction by reporting the direction the wind is blowing from.

To make a weather vane, which indicates wind direction, drill a hole in the middle of a stick about 12 inches (30 centimeters) long. Attach an arrowhead made of stiff cardboard or metal to one end of the stick as shown in Figure 75. (The easiest way to do this is to use a saw to make a slit in the stick.) To the other end attach a larger piece of cardboard or metal to form the tail of the weather vane. Drill a hole in the center of the stick (see Figure 75). Use a nail to fasten the stick to an upright stake or post. Don't pound the nail down too far since the arrow-shaped stick must be free to turn. A metal washer placed on the nail between the stake and stick will make it easier for the weather vane to turn.

If you place the weather vane on the beach, it will be a simple matter to observe wind direction. Why do you think a device that shows wind direction is called a weather vane? Hint: Is there any relationship between wind direction and approaching storms in the part of the country in which you live?

145

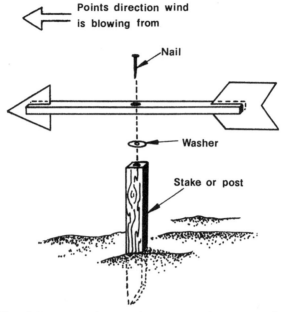

Points direction wind
is blowing from

Nail

Washer

Stake or post

Figure 75. A homemade weathervane points toward the direction the wind is blowing from.

If you don't know the directions at the place you are doing your investigations, refer back to the investigation on wave direction on page 91.

A device for measuring wind speed can be constructed easily, as shown in Figure 76. Attach a board (or a piece of stiff cardboard) about 12 inches (30 centimeters) square to a stake. Drill a hole near one end of a lightweight stick about 10 inches (25 centimeters) long. Or, for a more sensitive instrument, use a piece of stiff cardboard with a piece of soda straw taped to one end. Use a nail to attach the stick or piece of cardboard to the board as shown in Figure 76. Place

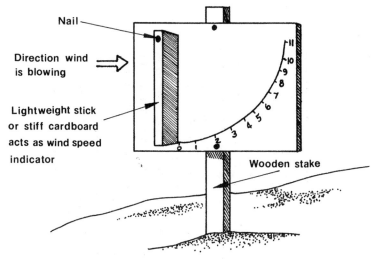

Figure 76. A homemade wind speed indicator.

a pencil on the lower end of the stick or cardboard and rotate it to make a curved line. Make marks 1 inch (2.5 centimeters) apart on the curved line. Number the bottom mark "0," the next one going up "1," and so on. This way your homemade wind speed indicator will indicate "zero" when the wind is not blowing.

If you want to record wind speed in miles per hour, there is an easy way to make an estimate. Look around you. Can you feel the wind on your face? Are the trees moving? Is a flag just hanging or is it being forced outward from the pole by the wind? Airplane pilots, boaters, and others who need to judge wind speed use the Beaufort wind scale. Try using the Beaufort wind scale in Table 3 the next time you are out-of-doors.

Table 3
BEAUFORT WIND SCALE

Beaufort number	Name	Miles per Hour	Kilometers per Hour	Effects
0	Calm	less than 1	less than 1	Calm; smoke rises vertically.
1	Light Air	1–3	1–5	Weather vanes inactive; smoke drifts with air.
2	Light Breeze	4–7	6–11	Weather vanes active; wind felt on face; leaves rustle.
3	Gentle Breeze	8–12	12–19	Leaves and small twigs move; light flags extend.
4	Moderate Breeze	13–18	20–28	Small branches sway; dust and loose paper blow about.
5	Fresh Breeze	19–24	29–38	Small trees sway; waves break on inland waters.
6	Strong Breeze	25–31	39–49	Large branches sway; umbrellas difficult to use.
7	Moderate Gale	32–38	50–61	Whole trees sway; difficult to walk against wind.
8	Fresh Gale	39–46	62–74	Twigs broken off trees; walking against wind very difficult.
9	Strong Gale	47–54	75–88	Slight damage to buildings; shingles blown off roof.
10	Whole Gale	55–63	89–102	Trees uprooted; considerable damage to buildings.
11	Storm	64–73	103–117	Widespread damage; very rare occurrence.
12–17	Hurricane	74 and above	more than 117	Violent destruction.

In studying wind conditions along the shoreline of a lake or the ocean it is important to get measurements of water temperature, air temperature, soil temperature, wind direction, and wind speed. A reading every hour is about the right time interval. The readings in Table 4 were taken on a beach in North Carolina and are reported for two-hour intervals to save space. Temperatures were measured in Fahrenheit and distances measured in feet and inches since that was the kind of equipment available.

Table 4

OBSERVATIONS MADE ON AN EAST-FACING BEACH IN NORTH CAROLINA ON AUGUST 3, 1976.

	6:00 A.M.	8:00 A.M.	10:00 A.M.	12:00 (Noon)	2:00 P.M.
Water Temperature (near the surface in water about 3 feet deep)	76°F	76°F	76°F	76°F	76°F
Air temperature (in shade about 4 feet above the ground)	73°F	76°F	78°F	82°F	86°F
Sand temperature (on the beach at depth of 2 inches)	75°F	78°F	81°F	87°F	92°F
Wind speed (in miles per hour; estimated using Beaufort wind scale)	0	less than 1	6–8	12–15	19–24
Wind direction	–	variable	generally east	east	east

If you have only one thermometer, take the water temperature on the hour, the air temperature five minutes past the hour, the soil temperature ten minutes past the hour, and so on. Be sure to take the readings in the same order each time and in the same way. For example, the air temperatures reported in Table 4 were taken at 4 feet above the ground and the water temperature in about 3 feet of water.

What does the data in Table 4 tell us? First look at the temperatures of the water, air, and sand at 6:00 A.M. As you can see, the air and sand are slightly cooler than the water. You also can see that the sun warms the air and sand while the temperature of the water stays the same. This is because it takes more heat to warm up some water than it does to warm up an equal amount of air or sand. If you don't believe it, try it. Be sure the containers (tin cans, plastic milk jugs, etc.) you use are the same size. Also the contents (air, water, sand) must be the same temperature when you begin the experiment. Set the three containers where the sun will strike them and record their temperatures at regular intervals. Which warms up the most? The least?

Look again at Table 4, at the situation at 2:00 P.M. The sand is much warmer than the water. Probably you know that air tends to rise above warm objects and settle over cooler ones. For example, the smoke rises up the chimney when there is a fire in a fireplace.

Figure 77 shows what often happens during the daytime along the shores of a large lake or the ocean. The air rises above the warmer land and settles over the cooler water. The resulting circulation of air causes

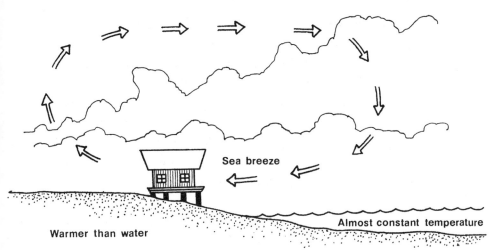

Sea breeze

Almost constant temperature

Warmer than water

Figure 77.   In the daytime the air rises over the land and settles over the water, setting up a circulation pattern called a sea breeze.

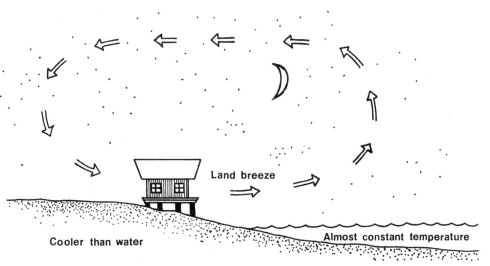

Land breeze

Almost constant temperature

Cooler than water

Figure 78.   At night the air rises over the water and settles over the land, setting up a circulation pattern called a land breeze.

a *sea breeze*, which is a wind that blows from the sea and toward the land.

At night the situation may be reversed, as shown in Figure 78. The water is warmer than the land because substances like water that are slower to warm up also cool off at a slower rate than substances like air and sand. At night the air rises above the warmer water and settles over the cooler land. The winds produced, which are called *land breezes*, blow from the land and toward the sea.

Even if you take measurements for the biggest part of a twenty-four-hour period, you may not get data exactly like that in Table 4. And you may not be able to observe sea breezes in the daytime and land breezes at night. There are many things involved in explaining the results you do observe. Major weather systems moving through your part of the country will affect the local weather conditions you are observing. Cloudy weather usually means lower temperatures during daylight hours and higher temperatures than usual at night. The time of year you make your observations will also be a factor.

In doing this investigation, you have learned about an important principle of weather science. Air, water, and the land warm up and cool off at different rates. As the result of this uneven heating and cooling, air movements in the form of winds are produced. This is the basic cause of all the weather on our planet. Different parts of the earth are heated unevenly and winds, storms, and other weather phenomena are the result.

HOW SALTY IS THE SEA?

Interested in an investigation you can do on a rainy day at the beach? Determining how much salt there is in sea water makes a good one. All you need is a sample of salt water and some simple equipment. You can do your experiments in the kitchen or on the back porch.

Scientists often need to find out how salty a certain part of the ocean is. Or they want to find out much of the various kinds of minerals are present in the waters of a lake or stream. Later you will find out how they use this information in their research.

Since the waters of the oceans contain more dissolved material than the water from lakes and streams, let's work with a sample of salt water. One method of determining the salt content involves weighing a sample and then letting the water evaporate. Any salts and other minerals are left behind and then can be weighed. From this data the percent of salt in the water can be calculated. The following example shows how this works.

One hundred pounds (45 kilograms) of salt water from the ocean is placed in an uncovered garbage can or other large container. After several days the water has evaporated. The salt left behind is found to weigh about 3.5 pounds (1.6 kilograms). We say the ocean water was 3.5 percent salt. This of course means that in each 100 pounds (45 kilograms) of salt water, there are 3.5 pounds (1.6 kilograms) of salt.

The salt content of the oceans varies quite a bit, and this is one reason why scientists need to measure the percentage of salt. The average for all the oceans of the world is about 3.5 percent. Near a river mouth where fresh water is entering the ocean, the percentage usually is less than 3.5 percent. In areas of the ocean where a great deal of evaporation is taking place, the percentage may be higher than 3.5 percent. Do you see why?

There must be a better way to find out how much salt there is in ocean water than to wait for the water in a 100–pound sample to evaporate. One method that is easy to use involves applying what we learned in the first part of the book about floating. You may have seen this method used at a filling station to check batteries and the liquid in the cooling systems of cars.

A sample of the liquid from the battery is taken with a squeeze-bulb device. Inside the glass tube floats an object called a *hydrometer* (see Figure 79). The distance the hydrometer sticks out of the liquid indicates the condition of the battery. If the hydrometer floats low in the liquid, the liquid is mainly water and the battery contains little or no electrical charge. If the hydrometer floats high in the liquid, the liquid contains more acid and the battery is charged.

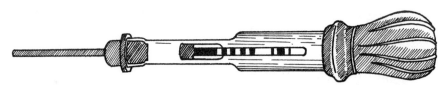

Figure 79. A squeeze bulb hydrometer like this one is used to test batteries and the coolant in the radiator of an automobile.

Using a hydrometer to test the liquid in a car's cooling system works much the same way. If the liquid contains a high percentage of antifreeze, the hydrometer floats high in the liquid. If the liquid is mainly water, the hydrometer floats low in the liquid. The hydrometer used for this purpose is marked off to show the freezing point of the liquid being tested. The higher the percentage of antifreeze in the solution, the lower the freezing point.

How can a hydrometer be used to determine the amount of salt in a sample of sea water? You can get a clue for answering this question with a drinking glass, some salt, some tapwater, and an uncooked egg. Place the uncooked egg in a glass of water. Does it float? Now slowly add some table salt to the water, being sure to stir as you do so. Does the egg float in the salt water? Does it float higher when more salt is added?

What you have observed about the egg should help you see how a hydrometer can be used to find out how much salt there is in a sample of sea water. The more salt in the water, the higher the hydrometer floats.

A hydrometer for testing salt water can be made using a plastic soda straw. One that is about ½ inch (0.6 centimeters) in diameter and 8 inches (20 centimeters) long works fine. You also will need a stove bolt about ½ inch (0.6 centimeters) in diameter and ½ inch (0.6 centimeters) long plus a wooden plug to fit into the other end of the straw. Screw the stove bolt into one end of the straw as shown in Figure 80.

Place the straw in a bottle full of plain water. The

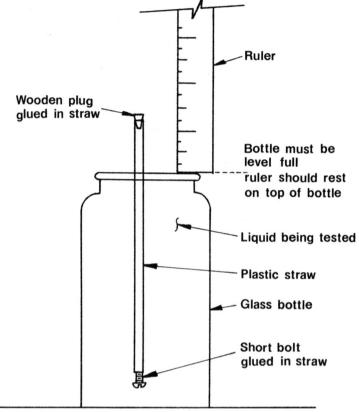

Figure 80. This homemade hydrometer can be used to determine the amount of salt in a sample of sea water.

straw should stick out of the bottle about an inch (2.5 centimeters). If the straw sticks out much more than this, use a longer bolt. By varying the length of the bolt, you are varying the weight of the bolt and thus the depth at which your homemade hydrometer floats.

Once you have the hydrometer adjusted so it floats an inch or so out of the water, remove it from the water. Take it apart and dry the parts. Place a drop or two of waterproof glue on the stove bolt and replace it in the soda straw. Glue a small wooden plug in the other end of the straw. Both ends of your soda-straw hydrometer must be watertight; otherwise the soda straw will fill with water and sink to the bottom of the bottle.

Once the glue is dry, again place the hydrometer in a bottle full of plain water. Carefully measure how far it sticks out of the water by placing a ruler on top of the bottle as shown in Figure 80. Be sure the water is level with the top of the bottle. Record your measurement in a notebook or on a piece of paper.

Next place the hydrometer in a bottle full of salt water. Notice how it floats higher than it did when placed in plain water. You may want to measure how much higher it floats in the salt water. This measurement will not be very useful, however, since we don't know how salty the water is. What we need to do is calibrate the hydrometer.

Many scientific instruments have to be *calibrated* before they are used—this means putting marks on them so they can be used to make measurements. For example, the marks on a ruler or meterstick are a form of calibration. These marks make it possible to measure the length of an object by noting where the ends of the object line up with the marks on the measuring stick.

To calibrate your homemade hydrometer, you will

need to place it in several solutions of which you know the salt content. You can use ordinary table salt to make these solutions. Table salt, or sodium chloride as it is called by scientists, is the major salt found in sea water. Make your solutions by following the directions in Table 5.

Table 5

DIRECTIONS FOR MAKING SALT SOLUTIONS

Percent of Salt in Solution	Amount of Salt Added to 20 Fluid Ounces (600 Grams) of Water
1	1 level teaspoon (6 grams)
3	1 level tablespoon (18 grams)
10	3 level tablespoons + 1 level teaspoon (60 grams)
20	6 level tablespoons + 2 level teaspoons (120 grams)

In making up the salt solutions, it will be helpful to remember that 3 level teaspoons = 1 level tablespoon. Also, you can see in Table 5 that each teaspoon of salt you add to 20 fluid ounces (600 milliliters) of water increases the concentration of salt by 1 percent. Can you figure out how to make other salt solutions in addition to those listed in Table 5? For example, a 5 percent solution? A 30 percent solution?

To calibrate your hydrometer, first place it in a bottle full of plain water. The water should be at room temperature (approximately 72°F, or 22°C) since the hydrometer reading is affected by the temperature of the liquid in which it is floating. Measure how much the hydrometer sticks out of the water. Repeat the procedure using the various salt solutions you have made up. Record your data in the form of a chart like the one in Table 6.

Table 6
HYDROMETER READINGS

Solutions Tested	Height of Hydrometer out of Solution
Water	1⁵/₈ inches (4.0 centimeters)
3% salt solution	1³/₄ inches (4.4 centimeters)
10% salt solution	2¹/₈ inches (5.4 centimeters)
20% salt solution	2⁹/₁₆ inches (6.5 centimeters)

The graph in Figure 81 was made using the data from Table 6. Notice that the horizontal axis (bottom line) indicates the percentage of salt in the solutions tested. The vertical axis (up-and-down line) indicates how much the hydrometer stuck out of the solutions. The points on the graph were plotted using the heights recorded in Table 6. These points were connected by the straight line that passes near or through each of these points.

Let's take an example to illustrate how the graph is used. In a sample of salt water at room temperature, the hydrometer was found to float with 2 inches (5 centimeters) sticking out of the solution. What is the percentage of salt in the solution? Going across from 2 inches on the vertical axis, the sloping line is crossed

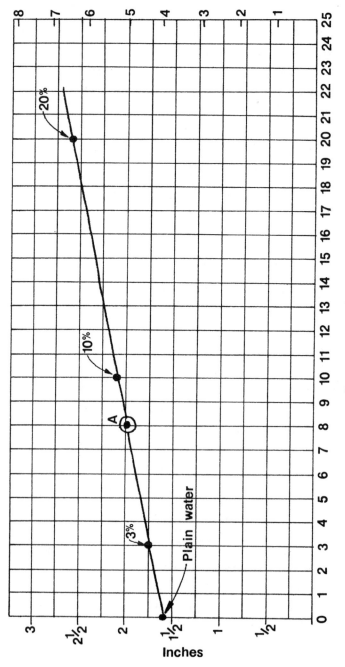

at point A. Reading down from "A" we see that the sample is about an 8 percent salt solution.

By now you have probably figured out how to use your own homemade hydrometer. Collect a sample of salt water of which you wish to determine the salt content. Place the hydrometer in the salt water at room temperature and measure the height the hydrometer sticks out of the sample. Compare this height with those in your graph, which is based on the measurements you made of solutions of known percentages of salt.

Perhaps you don't want to bother carrying a ruler with you to measure the height the hydrometer sticks out of the solution. It is often possible to improvise, as has already been shown several times in this book. Making a better hydrometer is no exception.

One way to redesign your hydrometer is to use a clear plastic soda straw. Before sealing the top end, slip a piece of rolled paper inside the straw. This piece of paper should have marks across it about 1/4 inch apart (or each centimeter if you are using metric units). The marks should be numbered starting with the bottom one.

When your modified hydrometer with the paper inside the straw is placed in a solution, you can read which mark lines up with the top of the solution. This hydrometer must be calibrated using the same method

Figure 81. This graph can be used to find out the percentage of salt in a solution. Go across from the height the hydrometer sticks out of the solution to the sloping line and then down to the scale on the bottom of the graph.

you used before. A graph similar to the one in Figure 81, which shows how the various marks match up the various concentrations of salt solution, will be very useful.

The next time you visit a store that sells auto supplies, examine the hydrometers that are used to test batteries and the liquids in cooling systems. You will see that these hydrometers have marks inside the tubes that stick up through the liquids in which they are floating. Also notice how the hydrometers have weights in the bottom that make the hydrometers float in an upright position. The stove bolt in the bottom of your homemade hydrometer serves this purpose. If you don't believe it, replace the stove bolt with a wooden plug and observe how the straw floats.

INVESTIGATIONS USING A HYDROMETER

Salt content is very important to most living things. Some plants and animals live only in fresh water. Others live in water containing more salt than the ocean's average of 3.5 percent. And thousands of others live mainly in marshes, bays, and rivers where the salt concentration may be somewhat less than 3.5 percent.

Figure 82 shows the Delaware River estuary below Philadelphia. In an estuary the fresh waters of the river mix with the salt waters of the ocean. Notice how the percentage of salt in the Delaware decreases as you move upstream. Many animals like those in Figure 82 are found mainly in regions of a particular salt concentration.

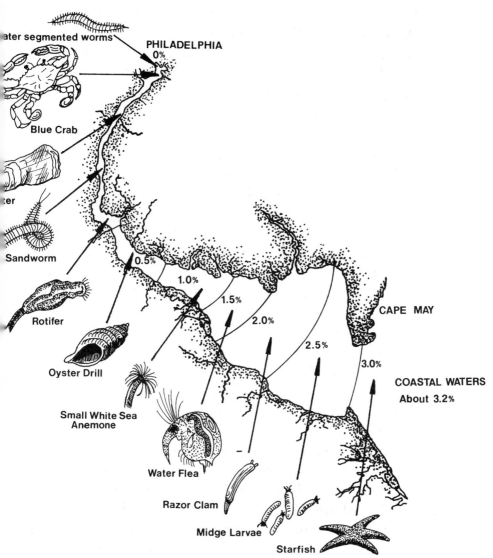

ater segmented worms

PHILADELPHIA
0%

Blue Crab

ter

Sandworm

Rotifer

Oyster Drill

Small White Sea
Anemone

Water Flea

Razor Clam

Midge Larvae

Starfish

0.5%

1.0%

1.5%

2.0%

2.5%

3.0%

CAPE MAY

COASTAL WATERS
About 3.2%

Figure 82. Notice how the kinds of animals found in the Delaware River below Philadelphia varies with the concentration of salt in the water.

163

Starfish live where the concentration of salt is about that of the oceans—3 percent or more. As you move up the river, you will find fewer starfish, but more clams, sea anemones, and oyster drills. The oyster drill is a small snail that attacks oysters. It cannot live in water much less than 1.5 percent salt. However, oysters can live in less salty water and those that live upstream where the salt concentration is below 1.5 percent are safe from the oyster drill's appetite.

Large changes in the salt content of the water at a particular place can have an effect on what lives there. This suggests the importance of measuring salt concentrations of the water if we wish to investigate what is happening to life in a given place. Here are a few suggestions to get you started on such investigations.

1. Is the salt content the same in water taken from the surf and water taken from a marsh?

2. How is the salt content in a marsh or bay affected by a heavy rain?

3. Does the salt content in marshes, bays, and estuaries vary with the tide?

4. Sometimes the water flowing into the oceans greatly decreases during dry weather. The boundary between fresh and salt water moves inland during these periods. Can you detect these variations caused by changing weather conditions?

5. Along some shorelines tidal pools form as the tide goes out. These tidal pools are like natural aquariums and often contain dozens of different kinds of organisms. On a hot day water evaporating from a tidal pool greatly changes the percent-

age of salt present. So does a rainstorm that adds fresh water to a tidal pool. Can you measure these changes in salt concentration? What effect do these changes have on things living there?

If these questions interest you, look in other books for ideas for more investigations. You may wish also to investigate the effects of other factors such as temperature, amount of sunlight, or clearness of the water on living things. The books listed in "Books You Will Enjoy Reading," on page 170, will be good ones with which to start.

Investigation of living things along a beach will depend in part on where you are and on the time of the year. But there are some activities that are popular everywhere. For example, most people enjoy watching shorebirds and collecting shells.

NIGHT LIFE ON THE BEACH

Don't overlook the beach at night. Many beaches at night are a beehive of activity compared to the daylight hours. As we have seen in an earlier investigation involving temperatures, the beach in the daytime can be a very harsh environment. In the summertime the dry sand can reach almost unbearable temperatures.

All you really need to study a beach at night is a flashlight. However, it would be nice to have both hands free if you are going to try to catch some animals. In this case a light such as miners wear fastened around their heads would be nice. Or perhaps you can team up with a friend—one of you holds the flashlight while the other tries to catch the animals.

You will also need a plastic bucket if you want to keep any of the things you catch.

It is a good idea to wear a pair of sneakers that will not be damaged if they get wet. Even with a flashlight, you will not be able to see as well as during the daytime. It is easy to overlook a sharp object or to step into a tidal pool.

Try to time your night trip to the beach for when the tide is out. Approach the beach slowly and with as little noise as possible. Raccoons and other large animals may be feeding on the food trapped in the tidal pools or exposed along the shoreline. The light reflected off their eyes will tell you of their presence. Often all you will see is their tracks in the sand.

You will be able to find ghost crabs on most beaches. Shine your flashlight at one as you walk very slowly toward it. The crab usually "freezes" until it senses some movement. Devise an investigation to see if this is so.

The shallow water along the beach contains many living things not found there during the daytime. A waterproof flashlight or one sealed in a clear plastic bag can be held underwater to reveal much of this life. Use a small dip net if you wish to collect samples.

The phenomena of "the glowing footprints" sometimes can be observed on a sandy beach in the summertime. To witness this you will have to turn your flashlight off. In fact, it has to be a dark night—if the moon is up, there is probably too much light.

Watch as a friend walks on the wet sand near the

edge of the water. Do the footprints seem to glow or light up a bit? If so, what causes this to happen?

Many animals that live in the ocean contain chemicals that cause them to give off light called *biolumines-cence*. This is the kind of light that gives fireflies their name. Some of the small organisms that live in wet sand produce bioluminescence. When you step on the wet sand, your weight changes the conditions in that part of the beach and the organisms are disturbed. The result is a "glowing footprint."

ONLY THE BEGINNING

Have you enjoyed doing the investigations described in this book? If so, the end of the book doesn't have to mean the end of your fun and enjoyment. In fact, getting the idea for an investigation can be half of the fun. And designing the investigation also is part of the challenge.

To get started on your own, practice being a careful observer. It won't be long before you notice something that will set you off on adventures of your own. Remember, it was two young people playing with a beach ball that led to this book being written!

Appendix

Metric units of measurement

Units	Equivalents
LENGTH	
meter (m)	39.37 inches
millimeter (mm)	0.04 inch; 0.001 meter; 0.1 centimeter
centimeter (cm)	0.4 inch; 0.01 meter; 10 millimeters
kilometer (km)	0.6 mile; 1,000 meters
MASS (weight)	
gram (g)	0.035 ounce
kilogram (kg)	2.2 pounds; 1,000 grams
VOLUME	
liter (l)	1.06 quart
milliliter (ml)	0.001 liter; 1 cubic centimeter (cm^3)

APPROXIMATE CONVERSION TO METRIC MEASURES

When You Know	Multiply by	To Find
LENGTH		
inches (in)	2.54	centimeters (cm)
feet (ft)	30	centimeters (cm)
	0.3	meters (m)
miles (mi)	1.6	kilometers (km)
WEIGHT (mass)		
ounces (oz)	28	grams (g)
pounds (lb)	0.45	kilograms (kg)
VOLUME		
teaspoons (tsp)	5	milliliters (ml)
fluid ounces (fl oz)	30	milliliters (ml)
quarts (qt)	0.95	liters (l)
gallons (gal)	3.8	liters (l)
TEMPERATURE		
Fahrenheit degrees (°F)	subtract 32, then multiply by 5/9	Celsius (°C)

APPROXIMATE CONVERSION OF METRIC MEASURES

When You Know	Multiply by	To Find
LENGTH		
millimeters (mm)	0.04	inches (in)
centimeters (cm)	0.4	inches (in)
meters (m)	3.3	feet (ft)
kilometers (km)	0.6	miles (mi)
MASS (weight)		
grams (g)	0.035	ounces (oz)
kilograms (kg)	2.2	pounds (lb)
VOLUME		
milliliters (ml)	0.03	fluid ounces (fl oz)
liters (l)	1.06	quarts (qt)
TEMPERATURE		
Celsius degrees (°C)	multiply by 9/5, then add 32	Fahrenheit (°F)

Books You Will Enjoy Reading

IF YOU HAVE ENJOYED doing the investigations in this book, you may wish to explore further the science that can best be learned in and near the water. There are hundreds of books on these subjects; those listed below are favorites of the author. Most of these books are inexpensive (the paperbacks are marked with asterisks) and many can be purchased at drugstores, newsstands and other places books are sold. Some of them should be available also at your school or public library.

Bathtub Physics by Hy Ruchlis. New York: Harcourt, Brace and World, 1967.

Golden Nature Guides. Racine, Wisconsin: Western Publishing Co.

    Birds by Herbert S. Zim and Ira N. Gabrielson, 1949.

    Fishes by Herbert S. Zim and Hurst H. Shoemaker, 1961.

    Pond Life by George K. Reid, 1967.

    Seashells of the World by R. Tucker Abbott, 1962.

    Seashores by Herbert S. Zim and Lester Ingle, 1955.

    Stars by Herbert S. Zim and Robert H. Baker, 1951.

Golden Science Guides. Racine, Wisconsin: Western Publishing
Co.
  Landforms: A Guide to Rock Scenery by George F. Adams
    and Jerome Wyckoff, 1971.
  Oceanography by Gilbert L. Voss, 1972.
  Weather by Herbert S. Zim and others, 1957.
Life and Death of the Salt Marsh by John and Mildred Teal.
New York: Ballantine Books, Inc., 1974.
  Life in a Tide Pool by William Stephens. New York: McGraw
  Hill, 1974.
The Peterson Field Guide Series. Boston: Houghton Mifflin
Company.
  A Field Guide to the Birds by Roger Tory Peterson, 1968.
  A Field Guide to the Shells of our Atlantic and Gulf Coasts by
    Percy A. Morris, 1973.
  A Field Guide to Shells of the Pacific Coast and Hawaii by
    Percy A. Morris, 1966.
  A Field Guide to the Stars and Planets by Donald H. Menzel,
    1975.
Waves and Beaches by Willard Bascom. Garden City, New
York: Doubleday and Company, Inc., 1964.
Our Living World of Nature Series. New York: McGraw-Hill
Book Company.
  The Life of the Seashore by William H. Amos, 1966.
  The Life of the Marsh by William A. Niering, 1967.
  The Life of the Oceans by N. J. Berrill, 1966.
  The Life of Rivers and Streams by Robert L. Usinger, 1967.
  The Life of the Pond by William A. Amos, 1967.

Index